Somebody's Daughter

A Journey to Freedom from Pornography

DVD Experiential Guide

By Michael John Cusick

Author of *Surfing for God*

www.musicforthesoul.org

©2014 by Music for the Soul, Inc.

Somebody's Daughter – A Journey to Freedom from Pornography,
DVD Experiential Guide
©2014 by Music for the Soul, Inc.

All rights reserved. Published by Cappella Books.
No part of this book may be reproduced or transmitted in any form or by any means, electronic or mechanical, including photocopying, recording or by any information storage or retrieval system, except for brief quotations in critical reviews or aricles, without written permission from the publisher.
For information write to Cappella Books,
P.O. Box 50358, Nashville, TN 37205

ISNB 978-0-9882870-4-4

Content Development Team: Michael John Cusick and Judy Gomoll
Project Coordinator: Tammy Stauffer
Internal Design: Christine Weddle
Cover Design: Heather Peters

Unless otherwise identified, all Scripture quotations in this publication are taken from The Holy Bible: New International Version (NIV). Copyright © 1973, 1978, 1984, 2011 by the International Bible Society. Used by permission of Zondervan. All rights reserved.

Manufactured in the United States of America

CONTENTS

Introduction 5

Somebody's Daughter ... How It Came Into Being 6

How to Use This Material 9

SMALL GROUPS

Session One: *Hooked* 13

Session Two: *Ashamed* 23

Session Three: *Desperate* 33

Session Four: *Exposed* 43

Session Five: *Relieved* 53

Session Six: *Freed* 63

Informational Groups 73

Vocational Groups 79

Your Brain on Porn 99

Recommended Resources 111

Introduction

THE STORIES VARY. But the problem is the same. Sexual desire—one of God's great gifts—gone awry. A wife walks in on her husband checking e-mail and discovers him viewing x-rated images. A veteran youth pastor is discovered using the church computer to download sexually explicit pictures and videos. A businessman travels out of town resolving one more time not to watch "adult" movies in his hotel room, but good intentions fall short—again.

Broken trust. Broken relationships. Feelings of shame and hopelessness. This is not the way it was meant to be. But what hope is there when committing to "just try harder" fails again and again?

Many are surprised to learn that compulsive struggles with lust and pornography are not really about sex. And they aren't simply about temptations for which we need to redouble our efforts. The critical issues are rooted deep in the heart:

For out of the heart come evil thoughts, murder, adultery, sexual immorality, theft, false testimony, slander. (Matthew 15:19 NIV)

The good news is that Jesus came to transform our hearts and to bring freedom to those held captive. Even better news is that God is in the business of taking the very struggles which have become barriers to knowing Him more intimately—things like struggles with pornography—and turning them into bridges.

Real change is possible!

Somebody's Daughter ...

How it came into being

FIFTEEN years ago my dear friend John called me one night and told me that if he didn't tell somebody his secret he was going to lose everything.

His secret was that pornography was threatening to destroy his life and his beautiful family.

From the outside looking in John would've been the last person you would have suspected to have a problem with pornography. He was a hit Christian songwriter, married to a beautiful woman, with two adorable young daughters, ages 4 and 2.

But on this night the mask was coming off. "I need to go to a sex addict's meeting and I don't want to go alone. Will you go with me?"

The following night that is just what we did.

When we got together the following week to process what we'd experienced we wrote the song *Somebody's Daughter*. It was our way of planting a flag and saying "From this day forward every woman we look at is somebody's daughter. They have a mother and a father just like our daughters. And they have a heavenly Father.

A few days later John wrote the song Free. At that point it was not a statement of where he was, but a statement of where he was going. At the time these songs were written, neither John nor I had any plans for a CD or DVD. For my own part I was just trying to help one friend save his marriage and his family and get free of pornography. The good news is he did.

John's decision to take the courageous step and reach out to ask for help led to the discussion guide you are holding in your hands.

Maybe you are the one taking that courageous step today. Or maybe you're someone who is walking with others, facilitating the discussion. Either way let me encourage you. Healing is possible. Freedom is possible.

The content here represents a labor of love and prayer. Having been present for both the creation of the CD and the DVD I can tell you the Holy Spirit guided every step of the way and we all experienced not a few miracles in the process.

When we started production on the CD I asked my friend Clay Crosse to sing the title track because of his own personal struggle with pornography, something that he had by then made very public. He told me he was willing but that he'd developed vocal problems while he was hiding his secret life and his voice had not come back yet to what it had been earlier in his career.

But the day he showed up to sing for us it was as if he had never missed a step. As he reached for the high notes the tones were clear and strong. We could not have hoped for a better vocal.

Later, as we neared the end of the recording process we couldn't get clearance for the speaking piece we had planned to use to introduce the song *Somebody's Daughter*. The day before our record was due for final mastering I called a therapist who was counseling men who were working to overcome a problem with pornography.

One man agreed to speak on the record as long as he could remain anonymous. When he asked what I wanted him to say I replied, "We'll just turn the microphone on and you say whatever you would like to say in your own words."

I didn't tell him the title of the project or the song that his speaking part was to introduce. So you can imagine how stunned I was when he said, "You look at your own daughters and your friends' daughters and you think, 'Wow! That could be the person that you were looking at and lusting over on the computer. Or your friends could be doing the same thing to your daughter."

The miracles were many. That's why I laugh when people say I produce these recordings. If only I could tell you how evident God's hand is in putting together critical moments like these. For instance, we had no idea that one of the men hired to shoot the video had a struggle with pornography that threatened to break up his marriage. Taking part in the DVD was a healing experience for him.

Here's another example. While filming the "Never Shake His Hand" music video, the film crew showed up to tape the scene where the house burns. When they scouted through the house to select the best location to tape they found the house vacant except for one thing – a huge stash of pornography in the closet. So when the house was set on fire to capture that scene the pornography went up in flames with it.

Most miraculous of all to me though were the interview sessions. The vulnerability and the courage of those who sat in front of the camera along with the sensitivity of the film crew combined to create something that is greater than the sum of its parts.

The stories of healing we've heard from those who have utilized the CD and DVD – of lives restored, of marriages and families saved – have been the greatest blessing imaginable and an answer to the prayers we all prayed during the creation of the *Somebody's Daughter* experience.

Michael John Cusick, a gifted communicator and teacher, has crafted an excellent resource in this wonderful discussion guide that will help further facilitate the healing of hurting hearts and restoration of depleted souls.

I pray the same God who shepherded the *Somebody's Daughter* project—the same God who delivered the men you will meet on these pages out of the grip of pornography and into the light—will now do the same thing for you or those in your care.

God bless you on the journey.

Steve Siler
Producer of *Somebody's Daughter*

How to Use This Material

THANK YOU so much for participating in the *Somebody's Daughter* video experience and for using this Experiential Guide. Many who have been touched by the *Somebody's Daughter* audio and video tracks experienced the life changing power of the music, lyrics, and video. *Somebody's Daughter* materials are being used around the world in church services, men's groups, Bible studies, counseling offices, college chapel services, and conferences. This guide offers practical suggestions for using this material in several structured ways, especially in small group and large group settings. We recommend that each participant in a small group have his or her own personal copy of this *Experiential Guide*. *Somebody's Daughter* DVD/CD set or additional copies of this guide can be ordered at: http://www.musicforthesoul.org/resources/somebodys-daughter/

Small Group Settings

The *Somebody's Daughter* video Experiential Guide is a six-week series designed to offer hope for the tens of millions who struggle with pornography. It invites you into redemptive conversations with others about the destructive impact of this cancer of the soul. The experiential guide sessions stay close to the content of the video and are flexible and user friendly. We offer three different levels of discussion questions custom designed for three distinct small group audiences:

Transformational Groups are comprised of men who are (or may not be) pornography strugglers themselves. They seek to help men begin the journey to transformation and freedom in the context of a supportive "band of brothers." These materials may also be appropriate for counseling sessions, focused men's retreats, or between a mentor and a mentoree. The emphasis is on deep disclosure and greater vulnerability, in settings where people trust one another and agree to carefully respect one another's confidentiality.

Relational Groups are comprised of women who are in a relationship with a pornography struggler. She might be the wife, mother, sister, daughter, girlfriend, or friend of a struggler. These groups have a medium degree of vulnerability, while honoring some degree of protection for the "man in her life" she wants to walk alongside. These groups seek to help women understand the struggler's journey better, and also to provide support for her own emotional journey through shock, anger, betrayal, etc.

Foundational Groups are comprised of men and women who want to understand pornography addiction and be equipped to walk with those who struggle. Low vulnerability is the norm. These might be staff development meetings, Sunday school teachers or youth workers, cell groups, Bible study groups, ministry teams, husband and wife, etc.

Large Group Settings

The *Somebody's Daughter* video Experiential Guide is also designed to help large groups process the journey to freedom for a pornography struggler. Questions and timing are custom designed for these audiences:

Informational Groups cater to larger public gatherings such as conferences, workshops, church services, college classes on sexuality, or college chapel. This will probably occur in one sitting over the time span of one to two hours. We imagine participants first viewing the video together in its entirety, and then discussing it for 20-30 minutes in smaller clusters of 4-6 people. Questions will not require vulnerability, but will certainly invite participation.

Vocational Groups are comprised of ministry practitioners and leaders, leaders in churches and non-profit organizations, or leaders and staff in business and educational settings open to a biblical perspective. It is also appropriate for those called to ministry, but not employed in ministry. Structured in two 90-minute-long sessions, vocational groups might use this material for professional development to help answer the question, "What do we do when there is a pornography struggler in our midst?" Your task is not to be the primary caregiver for a struggler. Rather, it will prepare leaders to respond appropriately and professionally to the first disclosure of an employee or staff member using pornography. It will also launch the exploration of current organizational realities (policies, penalties, support, etc.) and brainstorm possible strategies for handling this issue in the workplace.

A Word to Women

You might be surprised to learn that men aren't the only ones who look at pornography. We are very aware that women, too, are watching porn and becoming addicted—but hardly anyone is talking about it. This material focuses on men's struggles with pornography, but female strugglers will be helped, too.

If you are a woman whose husband, boyfriend, brother, father, son, or friend struggles with pornography, take hope. The insights offered here (under the sub-title "Relational Groups") will help you understand him better and encourage you to walk with him on his journey to freedom.

Al-Anon says this to the spouses of addicts: You didn't cause it, you can't control it, and you can't cure it. The same is true for anyone in relationship with a man struggling with pornography. But having said that, our encouragement is the same—there really is hope!

WHAT YOU WILL NEED

- *Somebody's Daughter* DVD with audio CD. If you don't have these materials, you can purchase them at http://www.musicforthesoul.org /resources/somebodys-daughter/
- DVD player suitable to the size of audience to play video
- CD player, MP3 player, or Smart Phone to play songs.
- An open heart

How to Use Your Time in Small Groups

Small groups usually devote six sessions to *Somebody's Daughter*. Each session is designed to last roughly one hour—or a little longer—and consists of a same format:

Check In	(5-8 minutes)
Preview	(2 minutes)
Watch	(7-9 minutes for small groups, longer for large groups)
Discuss	(20 minutes)
Listen	(4-5 minutes)
Discuss	(5-10 minutes)
Check Out	(5 minutes)
Digging Deeper	(Optional for later reading)
Total time:	One hour +/-

Session One:

HOOKED

CHECK IN (5-10 minutes)

BEFORE you view the video, <u>select one</u> of the questions below and respond to it.

- What brings you to this group today?

- What do you hope to get out of this session?

- Have you ever participated in a group like this before?

- What does it feel like for you to be here (relief, hope, anxiety, etc.)?

PREVIEW (2 minutes)

ASK someone to read aloud the preview of this session printed below.

Maybe this hasn't happened to you. But chances are it has happened to someone you know:

It has probably happened to you at some point. You set your heart on honoring a woman for who she is as a person—for the fact that she is "somebody's daughter." But then for reasons you can't explain, you find yourself caught in a familiar pattern of lust.

Maybe you've told yourself, "She's a person and not an object. She's a sister created in the image of God with hopes, dreams, and a desire to be loved and cherished." But still, you find yourself drawn to what is only skin deep instead of the person deep inside.

What in the world is going on here? Why do our good intentions fall short so consistently? An ancient saint once said, "Every sinful behavior is rooted in a legitimate godly appetite." Which means that beneath your lust is a godly appetite, a holy hunger, a God-given thirst.

> My people have committed a compound sin: they've walked out on me, the fountain of fresh flowing waters, and then dug cisterns—cisterns that leak, cisterns that are no better than sieves. *(Jeremiah 2:13, MSG)*

In the scripture above, God blesses our deep thirsts and desires. Including thirsts like intimacy, significance, and comfort—even sexual desires. Of course, only God's way can ultimately satisfy our thirsts. But predictably we turn away from God's living water and dig our own wells. Because they leak, we have to keep going back again and again.

So if you're asking, "Why do I see only flesh?" a better question might be, "What am I really thirsty for beneath the surface of my misdirected desire?"

WATCH (7-8 minutes)

WATCH *Somebody's Daughter* video: Part 1 from 00:00 to 7:15 minutes. Stop when Bernie (in rust colored shirt) says, "No one knew my deep dark secret." While you listen, use this outline to follow the key points and/or to take you own notes in the margin.

Notes and Key Passages

HOOKED

How does pornography affect men?

- One view says, "Porn is harmless ... Porn is just the way it is ... it doesn't hurt anyone, so what's the big deal?"

- Definition: *the graphic, explicit depiction of sex meant to stimulate and arouse*

- Definition: *porn is sexual images that (1) rob people of intimacy and joy, and that (2) paint a false picture of who women are*

- Porn makes a man feel alive; it says, "I want you! You're wonderful!;" allows a man to feel like a man without requiring him to be a man

- Porn is fantasy, fake, not real; it hollows you out vs. biblical sex which is real and designed to be enjoyed within the sacred covenantal boundaries of marriage

- Porn infects every group, culture, ethnicity

- Porn kills, destroys, strips men and women of dignity, violates love and prevents intimacy

- Boys/men might find it hidden in the barn ... shoplift magazines ... on home computer; begins as curious search and ends captivating them

- Paranoid pastor feared "someone will see me in the adult bookstore;" felt shameful. Nobody knew the deep dark secret.

DISCUSS (20 minutes)

REMEMBER that in this first session and all future sessions, you may choose to discuss all the suggested questions, depending on time. Or select only some of them, if that suits you better. Begin your discussion by reading this excerpt from the video:

In this segment, Michael (the narrator), John M (with wife Shelli), Bernie (rust shirt), and John C (businessman) share honestly about their early exposure to pornography and how it affected them. John M's first exposure came at ten or eleven when he found a stack of pornographic magazines in a neighbor's barn. Michael related being with a friend who stole a magazine from a store. John C. described working from home and discovering how to access porn from his home computer. What each of them quickly discovered was that they couldn't stop. Before long each man was leading a double life.

Michael (wearing a light blue shirt) says: *"We were created as men and women to enjoy the gift of sex and the gift of sexuality within a sacred covenantal relationship. Whenever we step outside of those boundaries there is going to be a diminishment to our own souls—it lessens our capacity to love and be human. Pornography strips men and women of their dignity. Pornography violates love and prevents intimacy—that's the case in my life ... it allows a man to feel like a man without requiring him to be a man."*

Transformational Group (FOR MEN)

1. Michael reminds us that, "Sex is in fact a gift from God." But many who struggle with pornography or other sexual sin say that it doesn't feel like a gift at all. It feels more like a burden or even a curse because of the shame associated with the gift. In the first 20-25 years of your life, what "messages" about sexuality did you pick up from other people or your culture?

2. How do you think pornography damages the dignity of women? . . . and the dignity of men?

3. Have you ever felt as if your sexuality is less of a gift and more of a burden? If so, how has this affected your relationships?

4. Have you ever shared with anyone the story of how you were first exposed to pornography? What is the story of how you were first exposed to porn?

5. How has this affected the way you see yourself or how you define yourself?

6. Do you agree that "porn allows a man to feel like a man without requiring him to be a man? What do you think is required for a man to be a real man with a real woman?

Relational Group (FOR WOMEN)

NOTE: In this Experiential Guide, we refer to "the man in your life" who is struggling with porn—whether it's your husband, fiancé, father, brother, friend, etc.

1. If you asked five women friends, "So what's the harm of men watching porn?" what answer do you think you would get? (Better yet, actually ask that question and record your friends' answers.)

2. How did you feel when the speaker said, "God has turned all that around [for us]"?

3. Michael Cusick said that, "Porn allows a man to feel like a man without requiring him to be a man." Do you agree or disagree with this statement? Explain what it means. What might it look like for the man in your life to step up to the plate and "be a man" in dealing with his struggle over porn?

4. How have you observed the man in your life's capacity to love being diminished by porn? (Consider both giving love and receiving love.)

5. These men told how frightened they were that their hidden, dark secret would be exposed. How have you seen secrecy and fear playing out in the man in your life? In your own heart?

6. Perhaps you have begged, "God, just take it away" from your man. Why do you think God hasn't "just taken it away"?

7. If you could read Shelli's mind, what do you think she was thinking or feeling when she first learned of John's porn addiction? Try to express this in first person: "I feel . . . ."

Foundational Group (FOR MEN AND WOMEN)

1. How serious an issue do you believe pornography is in our culture, and why? How serious an issue is it in your ministry or workplace?

2. How do you think pornography damages the dignity of women? . . . and the dignity of men?

3. In what ways have you, or someone you know, been impacted by pornography?

4. In light of the video, what if your teenaged son or daughter said to you, "Porn is harmless ... Porn is just the way it is these days ... It doesn't hurt anyone, so what's the big deal?" So what would you say next? What is the big deal about porn? Why is it actually harmful—not just a moral issue to a few people?

5. Michael says that, *"Porn allows a man to feel like a man without requiring him to be a man."* What do you think is required for a man to be a man to a real woman?

LISTEN (5 minutes)

WATCH and **LISTEN** to *Somebody's Daughter* music video/CD (4:40 minutes), co-written by John Mandeville © 2005 Silerland Music (Administered by the Copyright Company) ASCAP / Lifestyle of Worship BM

Somebody's Daughter

Words and Music by John Mandeville and Steve Siler

The moment she was born
Her mommy and daddy cried
Taken by the wonder of life
From Barbie dolls to ballet shoes
From roller skates to lipstick and rouge
She's become a lady overnight
Why do I see only flesh and look right past her heart
I try to tell myself I can't help what I feel

Then I remember

She's somebody's daughter
Somebody's child
Somebody's pride and joy
Somebody loves her for who she is inside
She has a mother and father
She's somebody's daughter

You knit her together
Your cherished creation
Made her body a temple for the soul
Why can't I appreciate
The beauty that your hands have made
And maintain my self control
'Cause when I see only flesh you're looking at her heart
There is so much more to her than meets the eye -
I need to remember

Heaven's own precious child
A person full of worth and dignity

When her beauty is defiled
I demean us both and fail to see

She's somebody's daughter
Somebody's child
Somebody's pride and joy
Somebody loves her for who she is inside
She has a mother and father
She's somebody's daughter
She has a heavenly father
She's somebody's daughter

DISCUSS (5 minutes)

1. Imagine the heart of a woman in the pornography industry. When someone looks past her heart and only sees her flesh, how does that impact her heart and soul? How does it impact the heart and soul of the man who is lusting over her?

2. Now imagine that this woman is your daughter (or sister or wife). What do you wish you could say: (1) to her, (2) to the men who view her in the porn, and (3) to the people who work in and profit from the porn industry?

CHECK OUT (2 minutes)

Very briefly, **RESPOND** to either one of these questions:

- What is one thing you'll take away from this session?
- Is there anything you learned about yourself during today's session?

Session Two:

ASHAMED

CHECK IN (5-10 minutes)

ANSWER either one of the following questions.

- Since the last time we met, is there anything you'd like the group to know about or pray for?

- What is one thing from the last session that you've been thinking about since we last met?

PREVIEW (2 minutes)

ASK someone to read aloud the preview of this session printed below.

> *Struggles with pornography or other sexual sin can stir up feelings of self-condemnation and shame. And like our ancestors in the Garden of Eden who covered themselves with fig leaves, we too hide our shame. With modern day fig leaves we cover ourselves by pretending, performing, and hiding.*
>
> *Shame can be a confusing and misunderstood concept. For starters, it is often confused with guilt—that sense of conviction we feel when we have violated some standard, when we have done wrong. So if a person lies, steals, or*

commits adultery, they will typically feel some sense of guilt for having done wrong.

But where guilt says that "I have done wrong," shame says that "I am wrong." Shame is a feeling (which often becomes a belief) that one is defective, flawed, unworthy, or bad. The lens of shame always focuses not on what a person has done, but on who he is.

However, as revealed in the amazing grace of Jesus, God Himself doesn't shame us. "Therefore, there is now no condemnation for those who are in Christ Jesus" (Romans 8:1, NIV). That's right. Jesus never shames us. Even though He knows about all the things we have done wrong, His heart toward us is one of kindness, compassion, and blessing. So whenever we are hearing the voice of shame, we can assume it is not the voice of God. Remember, God came searching for Adam and Eve, calling out, "Where are you?" Even though you may be hiding in shame, the truth is that God is searching for you, too.

WATCH (8 minutes)

WATCH *Somebody's Daughter* video: Part 1 from 07:15 to 14:25 minutes. Stop the video when John and Shelli are together and John says, "And we had to make that decision together." You can use the outline below for taking notes if you want to.

ASHAMED

How does shame impact those caught in the world of pornography?

- Sincerely didn't want to do this. Felt shameful, anxious dread, could never be wanted or loved because of what he did.

- Thought he could stay away from porn in seminary but addiction took root there

- Playing the part in church, yet filled with guilt. Tired of living a lie, leading a double life, experiencing no peace

- Outwardly everything looked like it was working, but inwardly porn affected reality, job, home life, self-respect, etc.

- In crisis and darkness he prays, "Just take it away!"

- Sets an impossible appetite and unreachable standard of marriage

- Women behind the camera in the sex industry are portrayed as saying, "I want you, and I've got to have you."

- But the women behind the camera really want to be beautiful and desired ... want unconditional love from one man ... are hurting and in prison just like the men who are addicted

- Enormous guilt drives the addict away from every relationship that matters (God, wife, kids, friends) and into withdrawal

- Affects the way you see yourself and each other

- Conflict demands resolution: pixels vs. real person

Discuss (20 minutes)

REMEMBER that you may choose to discuss all the suggested questions, or select only some of them, depending on your time. Read these quotes from the video to get your discussion started.

In this segment, each person relates that beneath a well-manicured life there was another life that no one knew existed. Behind an acceptable Christian veneer, there was a life of addiction, guilt, shame, and anxiety that was eating them alive. Read these excerpts out loud.

> **John M:** *If you had looked in on my life you'd have said, "This is working." We had the right car, the right home, a beautiful family. You'd see us at church on a regular basis. But the reality is that behind the scenes I had already departed. And once I began there was no coming back. Because of the secrecy it began to grow. As a result of it growing, the job was affected, my home life was affected, my self-respect was affected, my dignity was affected. All those began to impact my life.*
>
> **John C:** *I was playing the part, going to church every Sunday morning, sitting up in the choir loft, singing those songs, listening to those sermons, teaching that Sunday school class. But in the back of my mind I was filled with guilt. I was tired of living a lie. There was no peace. I had no rest. I was living a double life. And that guilt was driving me away from every relationship that mattered in my life. Number one was my relationship with God. Number two was my relationship with my wife. Number three, my kids, and my friends. Guilt had caused me to withdraw from those relationships.*
>
> **Bernie:** *At seminary the addiction began to take root. That's really where it became the darkest. I came away from seminary still holding the secret, still realizing that internally I'm still really in crisis over this. There was a darkness to me. No one knew, and I didn't want anyone to know. So I go back out into ministry serving as a pastor, and the addiction really begins to emerge stronger.*

Transformational Group (FOR MEN)

1. Do you think pornography can really be an addiction, or is it just a bad habit? Explain.

2. Why do you think we tend to keep our sinful struggles a secret, rather than share them with others? How has secrecy played a part in your struggle with porn?

3. How do you think keeping your struggles a secret "ties God's hands" from bringing the healing and help that is needed?

4. Bernie continues to share, describing how frustrated he was in not being able to overcome his struggle alone: *"I wanted to change, but change wasn't happening. I said, 'God can you just take this thing away from me—just take it away! I'll do whatever!'"* Why do you think that God didn't "just take the struggle away" from Bernie?

5. What are ways that you have tried to manage your shame and guilt (i.e., try harder, avoid thinking about it, blame others, etc.) How has that been working for you?

6. Is there anything else from these men's stories that you can connect with? Explain.

Relational Group (FOR WOMEN)

1. Sometimes we imagine that only certain kinds of people look at pornography—but "not *my* husband, brother, father, pastor!" After hearing from a pastor, a counselor, a businessman/church elder, and a Christian songwriter, has your perception changed as to who watches porn?

2. Would the man in your life say that his attraction to porn has become an addiction, or that it is just a bad habit, or something else? What would you say about that, and why?

3. In this segment, Bernie shares how shame urged him to keep his struggle a secret:

   Bernie: *At seminary the addiction began to take root. That's really where it became the darkest. I came away from seminary still holding the secret, still realizing that internally I'm still really in crisis over this. There was a darkness to me, no one knew, and I didn't want anyone to know. So I go back out into ministry serving as a pastor, and the addiction really begins to emerge stronger.*

   Why do you think the man in your life tends to keep his shameful struggles a secret, rather than share them with others?

4. In this segment each person relates that beneath a well-manicured life there was another life that no one knew existed. Behind an acceptable Christian veneer, there was a life of addiction, guilt, shame, and anxiety that was eating them alive.

   Select two or three of these things about the man in your life listed below. Describe in a few sentences how you think these aspects have been affected by his use of porn:

His relationship with God

His relationship with his wife

His relationship with his kids

His relationship with friends

His self-respect / dignity

His job

? Other

5. John M. describes some of the impacts on his marriage caused by porn this way:

    John M: *It sets an impossible appetite and standard. It steals from the true beauty of what marriage is supposed to be. It is the perfect theft of growing old together.*

    How does your heart respond to these thefts and losses? What is one additional theft or loss you have observed in his life—or in your life?

6. John M's wife Shelli sympathizes with the women behind the camera in pornography—although you might have expected her to be angry with them. She says:

    Shelli: *What she really wants is . . . She's hurting just like the men who are addicted to it are hurting. She's in a prison as well."*

    As a woman yourself, what would you want to say to the woman behind the camera?

Foundational Group (FOR MEN AND WOMEN)

1. Sometimes we imagine that only certain kinds of people look at pornography—but "not *my* husband, brother, father, pastor!" After hearing from a pastor, a counselor, a businessman, a Christian songwriter, and his wife share, has your perception changed as to who watches porn?

2. Do you think pornography can really be an addiction, or is it just a bad habit? Explain.

3. In this segment Bernie shares how shame urged him to keep his struggle a secret:

Bernie: *At seminary the addiction began to take root. That's really where it became the darkest. I came away from seminary still holding the secret, still realizing that internally I'm still really in crisis over this. There was a darkness to me. No one knew, and I didn't want anyone to know. So I go back out into ministry serving as a pastor, and the addiction really begins to emerge stronger.*

Why do you think we tend to keep our sinful struggles a secret, rather than share them with others?

4. Bernie continues to share, describing how frustrated he was in not being able to overcome his struggle alone: *"I wanted to change, but change wasn't happening. I said, 'God can you just take this thing away from me—just take it away! I'll do whatever!"* Why do you think that God didn't "just take the struggle away" from Bernie?

5. How do you think keeping our struggles a secret "ties God's hands" from bringing the healing and help that is needed?

LISTEN (4 minutes)

PLAY "Traitor" (audio track #4 on *Somebody's Daughter* CD, 3:07 minutes)
© 2005 Silerland Music (Administered by the Copyright Company) ASCAP

Traitor

Words and Music by Steve Siler

> I'm in church on Sunday morning
> Got the family and the new SUV
> Your co-worker and your neighbor
> I'm exactly who you think I should be
> But my eyes feast where none can see
> On visual profanity
>
> I'm a traitor
> A betrayer

A double minded-man
I'm a liar
A decay-er of everything I stand for
A voyeur in the dark
An adulterer of the heart
I'm a traitor
A traitor

I committed to be faithful
To keep my passion only for her
Now I'm surfing while she's sleeping
Trusting that our bed is still pure
I've taken what was intimate
And carelessly polluted it

CHORUS

I feel like I'm drowning
Out of control
Like an addict who needs a fix
Selling my soul for the counterfeit high
In these pictures and pixels

God I want to pray to you
But it feels like you wouldn't want me to

CHORUS

DISCUSS (5-10 minutes)

1. This song describes a man bound up in shame. How does this come across in the song?

2. "God, I want to pray to you, but it feels like you wouldn't want me to." How have you felt when you tried to talk with God about your struggle?

3. What would you *want* to say (not what do you think you *should* say) to the man in this song—the man who sees himself as a "traitor, betrayer, double-minded liar"?

CHECK OUT (5 minutes)

Very briefly, **RESPOND** to either one of these questions:

- What is one thing you'll take away from this session?
- Is there anything you learned about yourself during today's session.

Session Three:

DESPERATE

CHECK IN (5-10 minutes)

ANSWER either one of the following questions.

- Since the last time we met, is there anything you'd like the group to know about or pray for?

- What is one thing from the last session that you've been thinking about since we last met?

PREVIEW (2 minutes)

ASK someone to read the preview of this session printed below.

It comes to your inbox and pops up on your home page. It's in TV commercials and store windows at the mall. The reality of porn is everywhere. And like second-hand smoke, you don't have to be a smoker to be affected by it.

Struggles with porn and enticing images are indeed "every man's battle." But too many men are losing ground in this war. Often it's because they don't know exactly what they are fighting against. Or it's because they haven't been equipped to fight. Caught between the terror of being discovered and ongoing defeat, too many men hide their struggle and live in quiet desperation.

So what is this thing we are fighting? And how do we begin to turn the tide? As a starting point, we need to focus not just on what we are doing with our eyes, but also on what is happening in our hearts. Exercising self-control and having accountability are essential. But the primary battleground must shift from the outside to the inside.

"Keep vigilant watch over your heart; that's where life starts." (Proverbs 4:23, MSG)

Whether it's porn, an attractive coworker, or a private sexual fantasy, the real issue is never about what tempts us. The core of the struggle has to do with the God-given desires within our hearts, mixed with a self-centered demand for satisfaction (or relief) apart from God.

As we keep watch over our hearts, let's pay close attention to our God-given desires and to the ways that we seek satisfaction apart from Him.

WATCH (7-8 minutes)

WATCH *Somebody's Daughter* video: Part 1 from 14:25 to 23:40 (the end of Part 1). Take notes below if you'd like to.

DESPERATE

What does porn have to do with fantasy and reality?

- People who would never drive to an adult bookstore for porn can access it anonymously and "safely" on the Internet "risk-free"

- Teens and single men erroneously believe a wife/marriage will "fix" their addiction

- Porn use is not actually a sexual experience but a fantasy experience that the body gets trained for

- The reality of marriage isn't a fantasy—creates conflict with real marriage partner

- Now whenever life/ the reality of marriage is too much, he escapes through the door of fantasy porn—rather than running to God

- "I don't want this in my present/future marriage"—yet we will bring it into marriage; the habit doesn't go away with a wedding ring and rice.

- Fear: to be exposed for who he really is; being ashamed that others will see me for who I really am

- Terrified of losing his job . . . that his wife will leave with children

- Terrified that she will leave him alone to manage this problem that is already destroying him

- Wife is crushed, angry, bitter, disappointed →convinced she had to leave; he fears breaking her trust again and again.

- Terrified that he cannot connect with his own innocent child

DISCUSS (20 minutes)

REMEMBER: Feel free to respond to all of these questions if you have time. Or select a few of them that best fit your group. Read this material to get your discussion going.

In this segment each of the participants speaks about the risks he was willing to take by using pornography. With each of the risks came fear—and some potentially devastating consequences. Consider their words:

Bernie: *I was risking so much for pornography. I was risking so much for something so little. I was risking being seen by my children. What if? Imagine if my children were to walk in on their dad looking at pornography on the computer.*

John C: *It wasn't until one evening when I had my office doors closed and I thought my wife had gone up to bed. She came downstairs and opened the door, and there it was. As I think about that night . . . I remember the look on her face.*

John M: *I knew the degree of duplicity that I was living. So I just assumed automatically that she would leave. I assumed that she would say, "Okay, you're a loser" and "I can't believe this," which she did. But that also she would say, "I'm done with you and I'm taking your daughters, and I'm walking." And I was going to be left at this abyss to manage myself. I think that's why a lot of men don't say anything about it, because they think they will be left alone with something they already know is too much.*

John M: *When you are not married, you think that when you become married, this whole habit you've created will just go away, because now you will have a sex partner. You will have somebody there for whenever that urge comes up—you've got your "in house fix." But the problem is that it's not actually a sexual experience: it's a fantasy experience that your body gets trained for. So now, the reality—in the marriage—isn't the fantasy.*

John M: *You've got a habit built into your core personality, that whenever life is too much you escape through . . . pick the doorway. Whether it's alcohol or whether it is porn, or whatever it is, it's the release valve when I just can't take it* *anymore. As a believer, a follower of Christ, I should be running to God—not running to fantasy.*

Transformational Group (FOR MEN)

1. What are the risks that someone takes with behavior they're ashamed of like porn? What's at stake? Personally? Relationally? Spiritually? Professionally?

2. Why have you been willing to risk so much, even when the consequences are so high?

3. Many single men who struggle with porn believe that once they get married their struggle will end because their sexual desires will be satisfied. Many married men blame their struggle with porn on their wives. They convince themselves that they wouldn't need to turn to porn if only their wives were more or less _____ sexually (you fill in the blank). In this segment, however, John Mandeville describes how pornography is really not about the sexual experience. It's really not about sex.

4. Can you relate in any way to the idea above that "when I'm married I won't struggle"? Or can you relate to the married man who blames his own struggles on his wife's inadequacies or sexual performance? Explain.

5. Have you ever considered before that the issue of pornography isn't primarily about sex, but about something broken within yourself? John says that turning to porn isn't actually about seeking a sexual experience as much as it's about seeking a fantasy experience. What do you think that means? How true is that for you?

6. In what ways can you relate to pornography use as a means of escape, relief, or control for "when I just can't take it anymore"?

7. Consider these words from Thomas Aquinas: "Every sinful behavior is rooted in a legitimate godly appetite." If you agree with this idea, what might be some "legitimate appetites" beneath your struggle with porn?

8. What might it mean in your situation to be "running to God, not running to fantasy"?

Relational Group (FOR WOMEN)

1. What are the risks that someone takes with behavior they're ashamed of like porn? What's at stake? Personally? Relationally? Spiritually? Professionally? Other?

2. What do you think men are so terrified about if they are exposed?

3. Many men (especially teens and single men) believe that once they get married their struggle will end because their sexual desires will be satisfied. Many married men blame their struggle with porn on their wives. They convince themselves that they wouldn't need to turn to porn if only their wives were more _____ or less _____ (you fill in the blank.). To what extent do you think this is true? To what extent do you think they are just rationalizing deeper issues in their hearts, probably not related to their wives or even to sex?

4. What might it mean for the man in your life to "run to God"—not to fantasy with his struggles? What might it mean for *you* to "run to God," too?

5. Shelli described how she felt when her husband revealed his addiction. How did you feel and respond when you first learned about the man in your life's struggle? Where are you emotionally **now**?

Foundational Group (FOR MEN AND WOMEN)

1. What are the risks that someone takes with behavior they're ashamed of like porn? What's at stake? Personally? Relationally? Spiritually? Professionally? Other?

2. Why do you think men who struggle with pornography are willing to risk so much, even when the consequences are so high?

3. What would you say to a single man who assumes "when I get married, I won't struggle any more"? What would you say to a married man who says, "It's my wife's fault." What would you say to a porn user who says, "I just need to escape because I can't take it any more"?

4. Have you ever considered before that the issue of pornography is not primarily about sex, but about something broken within a man? John says that turning to

porn isn't actually about seeking a sexual experience as much as it's about seeking a fantasy experience. What do you think that means? What might it for a man to be "running to God, not running to fantasy"?

5. Consider these words from Thomas Aquinas: "Every sinful behavior is rooted in a legitimate godly appetite." If you agree with this idea, what might be some "legitimate appetites" beneath someone's struggle with porn?

LISTEN (4 minutes)

PLAY "Never Shake His Hand" (the music video from the video, 3:07 minutes)
© 1998 Broken Songs (A division of Killen Music) / Papa Goose Music

Never Shake His Hand

Words and Music by Rick Altizer

> Never shake his hand
> Although he asks you please
> Never shake his hand
> Or you'll catch his disease
> It's hard to gauge the power he commands
> You can never shake his hand
>
> Never shake his hand
> In the loneliness of night
> Never shake his hand
> Although it feels so right
> You must beware of the things that you demand
> You can never shake his hand
>
> Never shake his hand
> You're no match for his grip
> Never shake his hand

> You can't give him the slip
> It only takes one touch to understand
> You can never shake his hand
> Never shake his hand
> You'll find he sticks to you
> Never shake his hand
> He's something like the flu
> He's introduced as an honest man
> He'll recommend a subtle change in plans
> And then he'll leave you wasted in the sand
> You can never shake his hand

DISCUSS (5 minutes)

1. "Whose" hand is the singer warning us never to shake?

2. According to the singer, why shouldn't we shake his hand? Would you add any more reasons?

3. Is there any way that you might be "shaking hands" in your own life?

4. As you watched this video, what most caught your attention? What most moved your heart?

CHECK OUT (2 minutes)

Very briefly, **RESPOND** to either one of these questions:

- What is the most important thing you'll take away from this session?

- Share one thing you learned about yourself during today's session.

Session Four:

EXPOSED

CHECK IN (5-10 minutes)

ANSWER either one of the following questions.

- Since the last time we met, is there anything you'd like the group to know about or pray for?

- What is one thing from the last session that you've been thinking about since we last met?

PREVIEW (2 minutes)

ASK someone to read aloud the preview of this session printed below.

> On a typical day, most people have something in their lives that they would rather not share with others. Private thoughts. Personal struggles. Sins of commission and sins of omission. For the man who secretly struggles with pornography, however, being caught or coming clean is to be avoided at all costs. The price just seems too high.
>
> But if that same man ever hopes to be free of his struggle, telling someone else is a crucial step—one of the most difficult things he's ever had

to do. Having sin exposed is always painful, and much of the time feels like death. But in God's design, it leads to life.

If we walk in the light, as he is in the light, we have fellowship with one another, and the blood of Jesus, his Son, purifies us from all sin. (1 John 1:7 NIV)

Surprisingly, the real battle with pornography is not with our sin. The battle is about whether we will hide our sin or bring it into the light. If we stay in hiding, we're forfeiting the grace and forgiveness that is ours in Christ. Coming into the light plunges us into mercy and cleansing.

There is a temptation that is greater than sin. And that is to keep our sin a secret. To hide. To stay far from God and others. But because of what Jesus did on the cross, there is always somewhere to go and Someone to go to with our sin and shame.

WATCH (8 minutes)

WATCH *Somebody's Daughter* video: Part 2 from 23:40 to 41:38 minutes. Stop video when John Cozart (glasses and olive shirt) says, "Thank God I found my way out." Take notes below if you'd like to.

EXPOSED

Why must we tell somebody about it—for the man and for his wife?

- Strips men and women of dignity; tempts her to leave

- Makes her doubt that what they had together was ever real; everything feels fake and artificial; "Was I believing a lie? I didn't know who he really was."

- What he feels as shame ("I'm not getting close to you because you're purer than I am ... Please forgive me") she reads as rejection ("He doesn't want me ... I'm not sexy enough ... he's rejecting me.")

- She needs to know that it's NOT: "I'm being rejected...I'm not enough ... he doesn't find me attraction ... I'm not what he needs or wants" ⇒ feels defeated and wants to run away

- Myth to think he can control this on his own

- Core self-centered demand: I want all of my needs met—apart from God. That is the core element of sinfulness (wickedness) speaking.

- She's embarrassed, he's afraid, so nobody talks about it. Convinces him he's the only one struggling.

- Why must we tell somebody about it?
    - It needs to cause a major disruption in his life
    - Obsession with porn thrives in secrecy
    - Exposing it offers accountability and resources; he will need help walking through this. Without exposure, people sink deeper and deeper into darkness.

DISCUSS (20 minutes)

REMEMBER: *If you have time, respond to all of these questions. If not, feel free to select a few of the questions that interest your group most. Read this introduction before beginning your discussion.*

The overarching idea in this segment is the importance of exposing our struggles to someone else. Each man in the video said that it was absolutely necessary for him to make his struggle known to someone he could trust. And one wife, Shelli, speaks of what happened after "the bomb went off and the truth was out."

Shelli: *There's definitely a death of all that I thought I had and that was real. I felt like I didn't know him anymore. It felt fake, like everything we had prior to that was artificial. That I was believing the lie, that I didn't know who he really was, and the way he felt about me was a big lie. The most important thing for a woman to understand is that it's not you being rejected. It's not that you're not enough, not beautiful, or all that he needs or wants. That is so important for women to get. Otherwise they are just completely defeated in the fight. And it makes them want to run away instead of stand by him.*

John C: *By keeping my struggles with pornography a secret, initially we thought we were doing the right thing. Because nobody was talking about it in churches, I thought perhaps I was the only one that was struggling. My wife was embarrassed. She wondered what people would think knowing that her husband was struggling with pornography and had been for a long time. But I didn't know that as long as this thing remains in secrecy, that's where it thrives.*

Bernie: *The most powerful way for God to transform my heart and to change was for it to be known, and to be public, and to come out and cause a major disruption. My way would have been for God to simply take away the problem with pornography and not let anyone else find out about it. In this moment where I was so desperate I continued to hear God whisper to me, "Tell someone." So I said, " Okay I'll tell someone. There's one person I can call."*

John C: *When you expose it, when you start to talk about it, that's when you start to help people. That's when you start to offer people accountability and resources. But as long as you keep the lid on this thing, people are going to sink deeper and deeper and deeper into darkness.*

Transformational Group (FOR MEN)

1. Shelli gives us a look into her broken heart, warning other women not to blame themselves as she did. What might some women tell themselves when the bomb of betrayal goes off? How true do you think these self-messages usually are?

2. Each of the men in the video describes a similar pattern of hiding his struggle and never letting anyone know what was really going on. Why do you think that sharing one's struggle with pornography (and other habits and addictions) is such a difficult step to take?

3. John C. and Bernie both describe the time when their secret was exposed as the beginning of freedom and change for them. Bernie even acknowledges that his way would have been for God to "just take it away." Why do you think that bringing the problem into the light is such a powerful thing to do?

4. In the quote above Shelli describes the death of all she thought and believed was real in her marriage. What would it feel like for you to feel the pain and betrayal of the woman in your life (wife, sister, mother, daughter)? Describe how you think she would be feeling in her heart?

5. Bernie describes the process of the truth coming out and being exposed as a "major disruption." In what ways has/would exposure cause major disruptions in your life?

6. John C. mentions that his wife felt embarrassed about other people's reactions learning of his struggle. Have you ever held back from exposing an element of your struggle because you were not sure how others would respond? Explain.

7. John C. says, "As long as this thing remains in secrecy, that's where it thrives." In regard to struggles with pornography and sexual sin, do you think it is ever OK to have hiddenness in your life? Explain.

Relational Group (FOR WOMEN)

1. Shelli gives us a look into her broken heart, warning other women not to blame themselves as she did. How do you connect with her feelings? What have you been

telling yourself since the bomb went off? How true do you think these self-messages really are?

2. In the quote above Shelli describes the death of all she thought and believed was real in her marriage. To what extent do you believe the man in your life has really felt your pain caused by his secrecy and betrayal? Do you want him to feel your pain? Why, or why not?

3. Bernie describes the process of the truth coming out and being exposed as a "major disruption" in his life. In what ways has the man in your life's disclosure caused major disruptions in your life?

4. John C. mentions that his wife felt embarrassed about other people's reactions learning of his struggle. Do other people know about your man's struggle yet? If so, how have they responded? If not, how do you imagine they will respond? How does that affect you?

5. John C. says, "As long as this thing remains in secrecy, that's where it thrives." In regard to struggles with pornography and sexual sin, do you think it is ever OK to have hiddenness in your/his life? Explain.

6. What do you hope will happen if/when he exposes his struggle to trustworthy people?

Foundational Group (FOR MEN AND WOMEN)

1. John C. says, "As long as this thing remains in secrecy, that's where it thrives." In regard to struggles with pornography and sexual sin, do you think it is ever OK to have hiddenness in your life? Explain.

2. Shelli gives us a look into her broken heart, warning other women not to blame themselves as she did. What might some women tell themselves when the bomb of betrayal goes off? How true do you think these self-messages usually are?

3. Each of the men in the video describes a similar pattern of hiding his struggle and never letting anyone know what was really going on. Why do you think that sharing

one's struggle with pornography (and other sins, habits and addictions) is such a difficult step to take?

4. John C. and Bernie both describe the time when their secret was exposed as the beginning of freedom and change for them. Bernie even acknowledges that his way would have been for God to "just take it away." Why do you think that bringing the problem into the light is such a powerful thing to do?

5. Bernie describes the process of the truth coming out and being exposed as a "major disruption." In what ways do you think exposing a porn addiction bring "major disruption" into a man's life? . . . into the lives of his wife, kids, friends, and workplace? Do you think the price of this disruption is worth it?

LISTEN (3 minutes)

PLAY "Is It Me?" (audio track #10 on *Somebody's Daughter* CD, 3:16 minutes), co-written by John Mandeville © 2005 Silerland Music (Administered by the Copyright Company) ASCAP / Lifestyle of Worship BM

Is It Me?
Words and music by John Mandeville and Steve Siler

> I can't breathe
> This can't be happening to me
> Was everything we had just a lie?
> I believed while you deceived me
> Faithful while my love was being violated
> Nothing is the same
> Nothing to hold on to
> Where's the man I knew a day ago?
>
> Is it me?
> What did I do?

Am I not enough for you?

Is it me?

Was I wrong?

I believed our love was strong

Is it me?

I feel sick

Has it really come to this?

Didn't what we have mean anything?

You lied to me while you lay with me

What am I supposed to do with all the dreams you shattered?

How could you do this to me?!

I can tell you're sorry

Don't touch me!

I need you to hold me

Who's going to comfort me now?

You disgust me

I know this isn't like you

It's over between us

I hope you still love me

I hate you!

I hate that I need you!

Only God can save us

Only God can save us

Is it me?

DISCUSS (5 minutes)

1. You've just heard Shelli (from the video) singing about her shock and pain. What are ways you've seen a woman hurt by her husband's (or fiancé's or boyfriend's) struggle with porn?

2. Imagine this: A wife has just learned of her husband's secret porn addiction. A well-meaning friend tells her, "Well, you know, it takes two to tango" or "If you want to get your husband back, this book will teach you how to be sexier for him." What's your response to these kinds of comments?

3. For Men: Select just one of the questions this woman asks herself (see song lyrics). If the woman in your life asked you that question, how would you like to be able to answer her?

CHECK OUT (2 minutes)

Very briefly, RESPOND to either one of these questions:

- What is one thing you'll take away from this session?

- Is there anything you learned about yourself during today's session?

Session Five:

RELIEVED

CHECK IN (5-10 minutes)

ANSWER either one of the following questions.

- Since the last time we met, is there anything you'd like the group to know about or pray for?

- What is one thing from the last session that you've been thinking about since we last met?

PREVIEW (2 minutes)

ASK someone to read aloud the preview of this session printed below.

> *Imagine if you can what it would be like: No secrets. Nothing to hide. No fear of being caught. And no more wondering what people would think if they really knew your life behind the facade. What would that be like?*
>
> *Too many men can't even begin to imagine such a life. It seems more an impossibility than a genuine possibility. More a fairy tale than something real. But living with such authenticity, and the peace and joy that go with it, is the right and privilege of every follower of Jesus. To be fully known and*

fully loved. To be exposed in all of our sinfulness, weakness, and brokenness, and to still be wanted and valued.

How do we get to such a place? It begins by listening to that still small voice inside of our hearts. The voice of the Spirit. You know the Voice. The one that says you are more than the sum of your sin. The one that says, "Don't let shame define you, son/daughter. Let Me define you!" The one that nudges you to talk to someone about your struggle. The one that never stops whispering, "There is hope."

> The mind of sinful man is death, but the mind controlled by the Spirit is life and peace. . . ." (Romans 8:6 NIV)

Life and peace. It's not a fairy tale. And it's not a Bible promise that applies to everyone else—but not you. It's the life in God that you were created for. The only thing you have to do is take the risk of letting yourself be loved.

WATCH (8 MINUTES)

WATCH *Somebody's Daughter* video from 31:48—39:36. Stop the video when John says, "That's the decision we live with now." Take notes below if you want to. This outline is given for you to follow along and take notes.

RELIEVED

How does "coming into the light" bring relief?

- Speaking the truth with his own mouth helps him find a way out. Exposure → Relief → Freedom → Journey → Peace

- Sexual sin loses its power when exposed ... begins to break strongholds

- He needs help, someone he can trust and call

- Wife also needs someone to support her

- Not just accountability, but heart-accessibility

- Not just a cop or a coach, but find a cardiologist (someone concerned about the condition of the heart who will care, pursue, and probe)

- Count the Cost: the years of shame, lost opportunities, and wasted time. The Goal: to bring all this to an end

- Find community /people who care for you, who pursue you, who probe your heart (not just your behavior)

- Commit to becoming free; commit to fight this

- Draw the line for next generation; they will run where we stumbled. "This is the end! It stops here!"

- Go in with a battle mindset; determine not to be defiled/destroyed by the culture

- Decide not to be defiled by the culture and to do things differently ONLY by God's power

- Trust God to give you new eyes and new mindset

DISCUSS (20 minutes)

READ these quotes from the video. Then begin your discussion. Don't feel obligated to cover all the questions if your time is limited. To get your discussion started, read aloud these quotations from the video:

John M: *If you are at the breaking point then you are going to need help—even if it's just one person. You are going to need other people around you saying, "I'll help you walk through this. Call me before you are blowing up. Contact me before you do something you wish you hadn't done. Do this before you activate the shame in your life. Call me."*

Michael: *The biblical model is not just accountability, but accessibility. Where accountability crosses over to something really powerful to transform us, is when you're not a cop, you're not a coach, but you're a cardiologist. And a cardiologist is someone who is concerned with the welfare of my heart. Jesus said in Matthew 15 that adultery and sexual immorality come out of the heart. It's not what goes into a man that makes him do that: it's what comes out of his heart. So I need a cardiologist. I need someone who is going to care for me and pursue and probe and be willing to make an incision in my heart. So that when I come clean, when I open up, I'm not just going to sit there and bleed.*

John M and Shelli: *The generation behind us is going to run where we stumble. We made the decision. I remember the night we did. We held up our girls in diapers. I said, "This is the <u>end</u> of this. If I'm the only man who stands up in my generation, I will not take it anymore. It's worth fighting for." You know what? I'm not doing it all right. I'm not perfect. But maybe somebody will look back at me and say, "Great Grandpa John put a flag up while everyone else was out getting trashed and doing whatever they were doing." That Great Great Grandma Shelli stood up and said, "Women, here's your role in it." That's the decision we made. That's the decision we live with now.*

Bernie: *When I said it with my own mouth and spoke the story to him, I just felt such a tremendous relief and freedom. To finally be exposed and to let someone else know. From that moment on, it has been this journey of more and more freedom and more and more peace. As you expose this secret, dark, sexual sin it loses its power. As difficult and painful as it is to expose something so personal and so* *deep, it is the beginning of breaking the bondage and the stronghold that pornography can often have in a person's life.*

Transformational Group (FOR MEN)

1. Describe on a scale of 1-10 (10 being the most difficult and painful) what it would be like (or has been like) for you to expose something so personal and so deep.

2. Earlier in the video Bernie shares that God nudged him to tell someone about his own struggle. Have you ever felt that nudge? Why did you (or didn't you) listen to the nudge?

3. **Michael:** *"So I need a cardiologist. I need someone who is going to care for me and pursue and probe and be willing to make an incision in my heart."*

   What might it look like for a friend of yours to walk with you:

   . . . as a cop?

   . . . as a coach?

   . . . as a cardiologist?

4. John says he wants to leave a godly legacy for future generations in his family. When you think of your influence and legacy to the next generation, how does this impact the way you wrestle with your struggle now?

5. In relation to your journey with porn, what would you like your kids and grandkids to say about you when they grow up?

6. What else stood out to you from today's video?

Relational Group (FOR WOMEN)

1. In the secrecy of their struggle each of these men was alone. John M. stresses the importance of men asking other men for help in their struggle. Why do you think there is such a tendency for men to struggle alone?

2. Say the man in your life asks you to help him with his pornography struggles. What do you think it would look like for you to:

    . . . be a cop?

    . . . be a coach?

    . . . be a cardiologist?

3. In what ways do you need a cardiologist to help bind up the brokenness in your heart over this struggle?

4. Re-read Michael's quote above. When someone is trying to break free from the bondage of porn (or any other bad habit or addiction), why do you think it's so important to explore what's going on in his/her heart—not just in behavior?

5. Shelli says that the wife also needs someone to support her. What kind of support, specifically, do you think a wife needs? What if she doesn't get it?

6. John says he and Shelli wanted to leave a godly legacy for future generations. When you think of influence the next generation in your family, how does this impact the way you and the man in your life wrestle with his struggle now?

7. What do you hope your kids will say about him . . . and about you . . . when they grow up?

Foundational Group (FOR MEN AND WOMEN)

1. In the secrecy of their struggle each of these men was alone. John M. stresses the importance of men asking other men for help in their struggle. Why do you think there is such a tendency for men to struggle alone?

2. Before being exposed, each man in the video was deeply committed to secrecy, believing that somehow that he would be ruined if anyone ever knew about his struggle. Paradoxically, when their secret was finally known, they felt relief, peace, and freedom. Why do you think that exposure eventually brought such unexpected feelings like relief, peace, and freedom?

3. Another paradox is that a man first stepping into the light and having his struggle exposed often feels profound relief, while his wife and friends feel anything except relief! They feel profound shock, sadness, anger, or some other emotion. Discuss how being in very different places emotionally can impact relationships.

4. Say that a friend asks you to help him with his pornography struggles. What do you think it would look like for you to:

   . . . be a cop?

   . . . be a coach?

   . . . be a cardiologist?

5. Re-read Michael's quote above. When someone is trying to break free from bondage to porn (or any other sin, bad habit or addiction), why do you think it's so important to explore what's going on in his/her heart—not just in behavior?

6. What else particularly stood out to you from today's video?

LISTEN (5 minutes)

PLAY "Into the Light" (audio track #12 on *Somebody's Daughter* CD, 4:32 minutes), co-written by John Mandeville © 2005 Silerland Music (Administered by the Copyright Company) ASCAP / Lifestyle of Worship BM

Into the Light
Words and Music by John Mandeville and Steve Siler

> The walls are crashing down
> My illusion has been shattered
>
> Those thoughts that held me captive in my skin
> I've let the secrets out

I've felt the demons scatter
Maybe now the healing can begin

Into the light
Into the place where nothing's hidden
Into the light
Into the hope that I'm forgiven
Climbing from the shadows toward the way that leads to life
Out of the shame
Out of the chains
Into the light

There's going to be a cost
Habits that need breaking
I know the path I'm on will change my life
Oh God, I need you so much
Without you I won't make it
Lord, take the veil of darkness from my eyes

CHORUS

The unrelenting guilt that I've belonged to
Is finally letting go from deep within
Through the brokenness and tears
I've found its love I've feared
Yet love can take my heart from where it's been

DISCUSS (5 minutes)

1. Stepping into the light begins to relieve us from the shame and bondage to our pornography addiction (and other sinful habits). It also is the first step toward experiencing forgiveness. Discuss why you think it's important for us to

experience forgiveness from God . . . from others . . . and from ourselves. Which do you think might be hardest, and why?

2. The song talks about "climbing from the shadows toward the way that leads to life." In what ways do you think living in the light could be life-changing for the struggler? . . . for those who love him?

CHECK OUT (2 minutes)

Very briefly, **RESPOND** to either one of these questions:

- What is one thing you'll take away from this session?
- Is there anything you learned about yourself during today's session?

Session Six:

FREED

CHECK IN (5-10 minutes)

ANSWER either one of the following questions.

- Since the last time we met, is there anything you'd like the group to know about or pray for?

- What is one thing from the last session that you've been thinking about since we last met?

PREVIEW (2 minutes)

ASK someone to read aloud the preview of this session printed below.

> "Every addiction begins with a soft choice, a quiet compromise." Or it might be just the opposite way: "All freedom begins with a hard choice, a refusal to compromise."
>
> Your freedom begins one choice at a time. Over time, choices become habits, habits become passions, and passions become a life.
>
> Christ has set us free to live a free life. So take your stand!
> Never again let anyone put a harness of slavery on you.
> (Galatians 5:1, MSG)

I run in the path of your commands, for you have set my heart free. (Ps 119:32, NIV)

Arriving at a place of freedom reveals a wonderful surprise. On the one side of freedom is the idea that we are freed from something. We are released from pornography, or lust, or some other habit or sin. But then we discover that we are also freed toward something. Free to live, and move, and direct our passions in a direction that brings joy to our own soul and the heart of God.

Perhaps this is why Dietrich Bonhoeffer wrote that the pursuit of purity is not about the suppression of lust, but about the reorientation of our lives to a larger goal—a larger passion. You and I were created to live a much larger story than battling sin and resisting temptation. We were created for Love. And to make this Love known to the world.

The journey to freedom is a path paved with humility, perseverance, and lots of trust. Trust that God is bigger than your struggle, and that there's nothing you can do to step outside of His grace.

WATCH (8 minutes)

WATCH *Somebody's Daughter* video: 39:36—46:00. Stop video at the end. Take notes below.

FREED

How do we experience Gospel transformation?

- Beware of approaches that re-shame

- Jesus loves you radically and relentlessly at the expense of His own heart

- Jesus never shames you—even at your worst

- God takes your failures, sins, shame, wickedness, wounds to the cross—and transforms you.

- The cross is about more than forgiveness: it is also about entering into real life with God.

- Sets you free to love and live with your heart fully alive.

- God has to be bigger than this. There IS hope!

- Struggler: "God, I bring you my nothing." God: "All that is I made out of nothing. Today brings a whole new life for you!"

- Struggler: "God, this is so hard." God: "I know, but I am with you."

- Wife: "I don't have the right to hang on to my resentment because I was wronged."

- Struggler: "Lord, I feel so ashamed and guilty and ugly. I can't stand myself!" God: "My grace is sufficient for you."

- Gospel transformation doesn't have 3 easy steps. It's about letting God transform your perspective and give you entirely new values.

- The Freedom Cry (from David): "Show me Your ways, O Lord, that I can run in the paths set for me." (Psalm 119:32)

DISCUSS (20 minutes)

In a previous segment John Mandeville said that, "The only way to freedom is to commit to being free." In this segment each of the participants share how freedom played out in their life and what this freedom looked like as they walked from darkness to light. After reading these quotes from the video, respond to all or some of the questions provided.

> **Bernie:** *You have to go in with a battle mindset. I want to fight this battle. I want to win. I'm not going to be defiled by the culture and let it destroy everything that is so valuable and so important to me. This doesn't happen just because I want it to. This doesn't happen just because I know it's bad. It happens when I say, when I decide, "I am going to live differently. I'm going to do things differently." It is all by God's Spirit that this happens. You can't live differently and not have God be a part of it. My natural way to live would be to go and indulge, to look at every woman that walked in front of me and to seek out pornography. That would be my natural way to live. But God gives you that power. He changes you—He gives you new eyes to see with, a new mind to think with. And my mind and heart are transformed. There's constantly that lure . . . that call back into the other, dark way of living. But God comes in and He shows you a different way to live: to peace, freedom, happiness, joy, true intimacy, and fulfillment.*

> **Michael:** *Jesus is this amazing, radical, unbelievable, relentless lover who loves at the expense of His own broken heart. What that means is, at the center of God's heart, there's not shame when He thinks of me. When God thought of me in my darkest sexual moment, my greatest moment of infidelity, Jesus was not shaming me. Jesus was there on the cross for me. And the amazing thing about the gospel is that God actually takes our failure, our sin, our shame, our wickedness, our wounds, and He transforms it all. That's what the cross is all about. The cross is not just about forgiveness. The cross is our entry into a life with God, the God who embraces us, a God who doesn't shame us, a God who wants us, even in our darkest moment. And then He wants to set us free to live*

> *out His passion, which is to bless the world, to live with a heart that is fully alive to love.*

John M: *Even in the worst of it, I had a ray of hope. That God had to be greater than this, or why bother. So I brought my nothing. I felt like I had nothing left to give. I had no strength left, I had no self-respect left, I had no respect left with her. So I remember praying, "God I'm bringing You my nothing. If You can do anything with my nothing, and make a life out of it, I'll serve You the rest of my life." In response, I felt an impression from the Holy Spirit, "John, all that is, I made out of nothing. So today begins a whole new life."*

I think it's important that we don't paint an unrealistic picture and try to hand somebody three easy steps to a happy life. That's not what this is about. This is about transforming your perspective before God, allowing Him to give you an entirely new value structure. Men get so destroyed that they can't even run. They are fumbling all over themselves and applauding each others' failures. It's tragic to me. "Show me your ways, O Lord, that I can run in the paths set for me" (Ps. 119:32) was the cry of my heart. That's the freedom cry.

Bernie: *You feel like you just run out of all grace and mercy with God, where there is such shame and guilt and ugliness to your life, where you can't even stand yourself, and you wonder if God can ever stand you. I think the message that always came back to me is what Paul received—that "My Grace is sufficient for you." That no matter how far down this dark tunnel I travel, I can never go so far that God can't love me or rescue me.*

Transformational Group (FOR MEN)

1. After watching this video series, how would you describe the journey someone goes through from bondage to freedom?

2. The hope of freedom promises so much *more* than just relief from bondage. It promises a new life! For John to experience this new life, he had to face his "nothings"—then give them to God. Think about whatever you might be struggling

with now, or feeling hopeless about. What might it look like for you to bring your "nothing" to God? What do you think He would do with that?

3. Michael: *"...at the center of God's heart, there's not shame when He thinks of me. When God thought of me in my darkest sexual moment, my greatest moment of infidelity, Jesus was not shaming me. Jesus was there on the cross for me, saying, 'This is what I'm going to do to set Michael free and bind up his broken heart.'"* What stirs up in you to be reminded that Jesus is not ashamed of you—and He will never shame you?

4. Bernie talks above about making a decision to live life differently. What might it mean for you to do live life differently—different how?

5. Bernie: "No matter how far down this dark tunnel I travel, I can never go so far that God can't love me or rescue me." In the journey ahead of you, what is one thing that brings you hope?

6. *"I run in the path of your commands, for you have set my heart free."* (Psalm 119, 32, NIV) David was both the man after God's own heart and a known adulterer (to only mention one of his sins). Yet he proclaimed for all to hear that God had set his heart free. When you imagine yourself *"running in the path of [God's] commands"* and having your heart set free, what stirs up in you emotionally?

Relational Group (FOR WOMEN)

1. Now that you've watched the whole video, how do you understand a porn struggler's journey from bondage to freedom?

2. John's surrender to Jesus and resolute commitment to fight for her heart and their marriage is powerful to hear! What is stirred in your heart to hear a man offer that to his wife?

3. Walking with a sexual struggler involves dealing with the shame he probably feels about himself. It also involves facing the likelihood that you are probably ashamed of him, too. Michael gives us a glimpse into God's heart by reminding us that *"at the*

center of God's heart, there is not shame when He things of me." How does knowing that fact speak into your own value and worth? . . . and into his?

4. Here is another powerful verse about God's heart:

   "I run in the path of your commands, for you have set my heart free."
   (Psalm 119, 32, NIV)

   The man in your life will probably stumble again and fall . . . and will have to get up and run again. How does this verse bring you hope in the journey ahead of you both?

5. Bernie states, "No matter how far down this dark tunnel I travel, I can never go so far that God can't love me or rescue me." In the journey ahead of you, what is one thing that brings you hope?

Foundational Group (FOR MEN AND WOMEN)

1. After watching this video series, how would you describe the journey someone goes through from bondage to freedom?

2. What have you learned from the video about how followers of Jesus actually experience transformation?

3. Regardless of the natures of your struggle, share about a time when you have experienced transformation as a result of God's grace.

4. The hope of freedom promises so much *more* than just relief from bondage. It promises a new life! For John to experience this new life, he had to face his "nothings"—and then give them to God. Think about whatever you might be struggling with now, or feeling hopeless about. What might it look like for you to bring your "nothing" to God? What do you think He would do it that?

5. *"I run in the path of your commands, for you have set my heart free."* (Psalm 119, 32, NIV) Jesus paid for the freedom of every believer. Freedom is more than relief from bondage. It's also freedom to move *toward* something. If you stepped into the next level of freedom that God has for you, how would your life look different?

6. In light of all you have learned and experienced during *Somebody's Daughter*, what are the next couple of steps for you?

LISTEN (5 minutes)

WATCH "Free" music video, by John Mandeville. (4:31 minutes).

© 2005 Lifestyle of Worship (Administered by the Copyright Company) ASCAP / Lifestyle of Worship BMI

Free

Words and Music by John Mandeville

>I'm not fighting anymore
>I stopped trying
>Yeah I've burned all the ammunition
>That kept me at war
>I'm not weary anymore
>I've stopped trying
>Trying to live up to expectations
>That weren't even mine
>
>I'm free
>Finally free
>Oh I'm free from the pain and confusion
>Thought I'd never be
>Yeah I'm free
>So free
>
>Made my way through the lies and delusion
>To this sweet release
>I'm free
>
>I'm not tortured anymore
>Got no secrets

I've come clean with the dark obsessions
That haunted my life

I'm not lonely anymore
I've stopped hiding
Yeah I've opened my heart to the passion
That burns in your eyes

CHORUS

And I can't explain
What you've done for me baby
With a love that dared to believe
With a love that really believes

DISCUSS (5 minutes)

1. To find freedom from the power of porn, most men tell themselves to "try harder." Yet John sings that he "stopped trying." What do you think that means? Whatever you struggle with, what would it look like for you to stop trying harder in order to find freedom?

2. What part does love play in a man's journey to freedom?

3. If Jesus on the cross could speak directly to the porn struggler, what are 3-4 things you believe He might say?

CHECK OUT (2 minutes)

Very briefly, RESPOND to this question:

- What is one impacting thing you'll take away from your group experience with the *Somebody's Daughter* material?

INFORMATIONAL GROUP

(for medium—large groups, public settings, etc.)

If your context is a large group or you are devoting only one 60-90-minute session to the Somebody's Daughter video, we suggest this plan for getting the most out of your experience.

PREVIEW (2 minutes)

ASK someone to read aloud this brief preview:

The stories vary. But the problem is the same. Sexual desire—one of God's great gifts—gone awry. A wife walks in on her husband checking e-mail and discovers him viewing x-rated images. A veteran youth pastor is discovered using the church computer to download sexually explicit pictures and videos. A businessman travels out of town resolving one more time not to watch "adult" movies in his hotel room, but good intentions fall short—again.

Broken trust. Broken relationships. Feelings of shame and hopelessness. This is not the way it was meant to be. But what hope is there when committing to "just try harder" fails again and again?

Many are surprised to learn that compulsive struggles with lust and pornography are not really about sex. And they aren't simply about temptations for which we need to redouble our efforts. The critical issues are rooted deep in the heart:

> For out of the heart come evil thoughts, murder, adultery, sexual immorality, theft, false testimony, slander. *(Matthew 15:19 NIV)*

The good news is that Jesus came to transform our hearts and to bring freedom to those held captive. Even better news is that God is in the business of taking the very struggles that have become barriers to knowing Him more intimately—things like struggles with pornography—and turning them into bridges.

Real change is possible!

WATCH (4-6 minutes)

VIEW the entire *Somebody's Daughter* video. An outline-summary of the video is available in the next chapter.

DISCUSS (Optional) (15-30 minutes)

IN your small groups of 4-5, discuss the following questions together.

1. What stood out to you from the video? Or what new insights did you gain about the struggle with pornography?

2. What were you aware of feeling at various points during the program?

3. What questions do you have that you would like your group to discuss?

4. How do you think what you've learned today might help you or someone you know?

MUSIC (5 minutes)

WATCH and LISTEN to the song "Somebody's Daughter" music video (4:40 minutes), co-written by John Mandeville © 2005 Silerland Music (Administered by the Copyright Company) ASCAP / Lifestyle of Worship BM

Somebody's Daughter

Words and Music by John Mandeville and Steve Siler

The moment she was born
Her mommy and daddy cried
Taken by the wonder of life
From Barbie dolls to ballet shoes
From roller skates to lipstick and rouge
She's become a lady overnight
Why do I see only flesh and look right past her heart
I try to tell myself I can't help what I feel

Then I remember

She's somebody's daughter
Somebody's child
Somebody's pride and joy
Somebody loves her for who she is inside
She has a mother and father
She's somebody's daughter

You knit her together
Your cherished creation
Made her body a temple for the soul
Why can't I appreciate
The beauty that your hands have made
And maintain my self control
'Cause when I see only flesh you're looking at her heart
There is so much more to her than meets the eye -
I need to remember

Heaven's own precious child
A person full of worth and dignity

When her beauty is defiled
I demean us both and fail to see

She's somebody's daughter
Somebody's child
Somebody's pride and joy
Somebody loves her for who she is inside
She has a mother and father
She's somebody's daughter
She has a heavenly father
She's somebody's daughter

DIGGING DEEPER

MANY of the ideas and concepts about why men struggle with porn and how God leads men to wholeness and freedom are discussed in more depth in Michael John Cusick's book, *Surfing for God: Discovering the Divine Desire Beneath Sexual Struggle,* (Thomas Nelson, 2012).

"This is a dangerous and beautiful book, filled with courage, filled with hope. This book will set you free. The process Michael describes here works—I've seen it happen with many men. That's why you should read this book. Then give it to every man you know." –John Eldredge, author of *Wild at Heart* and *Beautiful Outlaw*

VOCATIONAL GROUP

(for ministry practitioners, counselors, leaders in businesses, educational organizations, and churches)

GROUP PREPARATION

IF your context is a small or large group of participants from the fields of business, ministry, education, or counseling, we suggest processing this material as part of professional development. It will prepare leaders and staff to respond appropriately and professionally to the first disclosure of an employee or staff member using pornography. It will also launch the exploration of current organizational realities (policies, penalties, support, etc.) and brainstorm possible strategies for handling this issue in the workplace.

Part 1 (90-minutes) will help you (and your group) answer the question, "What do we do when it comes to our attention that someone in our organization is struggling with pornography?" You will also explore the experience of becoming hooked on pornography, as well as being too ashamed and terrified to seek help. It is here—prior to "the bomb going off" and your employee or staff member being exposed—that you can assess the current realities in your professional or organizational setting. You will have a chance to review your current responses, policies, penalties, unintended consequences, and attitudes to those struggling with pornography.

PART 1 (90 minutes)

PREVIEW (3 minutes)

ASK someone to read aloud this brief preview:

> "I need you to take a look at these," his boss said, clearing his throat as he pushed a half-inch stack of paper across the desk. He was caught totally off guard. Rob looked at the top page and immediately his face turned hot and his heart pounded like a bass drum in his chest. Slumping in the chair, he let out an expletive and sighed.
>
> Staring back at him was over six months of Internet history exposing his porn use on the company computer. The proof before him was undeniable. Next Rob's boss pushed a copy of the company's Internet usage agreement across the desk, which explicitly prohibited viewing pornographic material during company time and on company computers. The agreement, bearing Rob's signature, stipulated immediate termination for anyone violating the policy. Numb, Rob walked out of his supervisor's office, emptied his desk, and joined the ranks of the unemployed—all because of porn.
>
> The sting of Rob's shame ran deep. First, he felt the shame of looking at porn—the embarrassment at being caught, the humiliation of being fired from his job, and mortification at the thought of having to tell his wife that he was fired . . . and why.—Story taken from Surfing for God: Discovering the Divine Desire Beneath Sexual Struggle, by Michael John Cusick, page 66.

....

The stories vary. But the problem is the same. Sexual desire—one of God's great gifts—gone awry. A wife walks in on her husband checking e-mail and discovers him viewing x-rated images. A veteran youth pastor is discovered using the church computer to download sexually explicit pictures and videos. A *businessman travels out of town resolving one more time not to watch "adult" movies in his hotel room, but good intentions fall short—again.*

Broken trust. Broken relationships. Feelings of shame and hopelessness. This is not the way it was meant to be. But what hope is there when committing to "just try harder" fails again and again?

Many are surprised to learn that compulsive struggles with lust and pornography are not really about sex. And they aren't simply about temptations for which we need to redouble our efforts. The critical issues are rooted deep in the heart:

> For out of the heart come evil thoughts, murder, adultery,
> sexual immorality, theft, false testimony, slander.
> (Matthew 15:19 NIV)

The good news is that Jesus came to transform our hearts and to bring freedom to those held captive. Even better news is that God is in the business of taking the very struggles that have become barriers to knowing Him more intimately—things like struggles with pornography—and turning them into bridges. Real change is possible!

CHECK IN (5-8 minutes)

FORM yourselves into small groups of 3-6 people. Take only 5-8 minutes to discuss any (not all) of these icebreaker questions (and the questions on your current realities) before you view the video:

- What brings you to this group today?

- Which organization or ministry do you serve? In what capacity?

- What do you hope to get out of this session?

- What does it feel like for you to be here discussing the topic of pornography (relief, hope, anxiety, etc.)?

DISCUSS YOUR CURRENT REALITIES (15-20 minutes)

1. In your organization or ministry context, in what ways has pornography impacted your staff and personnel?

2. What is the level of urgency felt in your organization or ministry about coming alongside those struggling with porn?

3. In just a few words, how would you describe your organization or ministry's actual response to or policy toward those in your midst who struggle with pornography? (For example: zero tolerance . . . restorative and grace-filled . . . confused and inconsistent . . . disciplinary and punitive . . . what policy?! . . . other?) Where are you in terms of actually forming a written "policy" or plan on this issue?

4. Where are your leadership and staff right now in terms of their preparedness and training to respond to pornography strugglers?

WATCH (24 minutes)

VIEW the first half of the *Somebody's Daughter* video (from 0:00—23:40). Using the outline below, take notes on particular things that touch you or that you would like to discuss later.

Notes and Key Passages

HOOKED

How does pornography affect men?

- One view says, "Porn is harmless ... Porn is just the way it is ... it doesn't hurt anyone, so what's the big deal?"

- Definition: the graphic, explicit depiction of sex meant to stimulate and arouse

- Definition: porn is sexual images that (1) rob people of intimacy and joy, and that (2) paint a false picture of who women are

- Porn makes a man feel alive; it says, "I want you! You're wonderful!"; allows a man to feel like a man without requiring him to *be* a man

- Porn is fantasy, fake, not real; it hollows you out vs. biblical sex which is real and designed to be enjoyed within the sacred covenantal boundaries

- Porn infects every group, culture, ethnicity

- Porn kills, destroys, strips men and women of dignity; it violates love and prevents intimacy

- Boys/men might find is hidden in the barn ... shoplift magazines ... on home computer; begins as curious search and ends captivating us

- Paranoid pastor feared "someone will see me in the adult bookstore"; felt shameful. Nobody knew the deep dark secret.

ASHAMED

How does shame impact those caught in the world of pornography?

- Sincerely didn't want to do this. Felt shameful, anxious dread, could never be wanted or loved because of what he did.

- Thought he could stay away from porn in seminary but addiction took root there.

- Playing the part in Church, yet filled with guilt. Tired of living a lie, leading a double life, experiencing no peace.

- Outwardly everything looked like it was working, but inwardly porn affected reality, job, home life, self-respect, etc.

- In crisis and darkness he prays, "Just take it away!"

- Sets an impossible appetite and unreachable standard of marriage.

- Women behind the camera in the sex industry are portrayed as saying, "I want you, and I've got to have you."

- But the women behind the camera really want to be beautiful and desired ... want unconditional love from one man ... are hurting and in prison just like the men who are addicted.

- Enormous guilt drives the addict away from every relationship that matters (God, wife, kids, friends) and into withdrawal.

- Affects the way you see yourself and each other.

- Conflict demands resolution: pixels vs. real person.

DESPERATE

What does porn have to do with fantasy and reality?

- People who would never drive to an adult bookstore for porn can access it anonymously and "safely" on the Internet "risk-free."

- Teens and single men erroneously believe a wife/marriage will "fix" their addiction.

- Porn use is not actually a sexual experience but a fantasy experience that the body gets trained for.

- The reality of marriage isn't a fantasy—creates conflict with real marriage partner.

- Now whenever life/ the reality of marriage is too much, he escapes through the door of fantasy porn—rather than running to God.

- "I don't want this in my present/future marriage"— yet we will bring it into marriage; the habit doesn't go away with a wedding ring and rice.

- Fear: to be exposed for who he really is; being ashamed that others will see me for who I really am.

- Terrified of losing his job . . . that his wife will leave with children.

- Terrified that she will leave him alone to manage this problem that is already destroying him.

- Wife is crushed, angry, bitter, disappointed →convinced she had to leave; he fears breaking her trust again and again.

- Terrified that he cannot connect with his own innocent child.

DISCUSS VIDEO (20 minutes)

1. What is your reaction to the words and stories of the people in the video?

2. CASE STUDY: Select one of the four men you've seen in the video. If he were employed in your organization or on staff in your ministry, what would be the first three tangible steps you would take upon discovering his hidden addiction?

3. In light of the video, what have you learned so far or what would you change about your organization's approach to sexual strugglers among you?

4. What is one question you have as a result of watching the video so far?

LISTEN (5 minutes)

PLAY "Traitor" (audio track #4 on *Somebody's Daughter* CD, 3:07 minutes)
© 2005 Silerland Music (Administered by the Copyright Company) ASCAP

Traitor
Words and Music by Steve Siler

>I'm in church on Sunday morning
>Got the family and the new SUV
>Your co-worker and your neighbor
>I'm exactly who you think I should be
>But my eyes feast where none can see
>On visual profanity
>
>I'm a traitor
>A betrayer

A double minded-man

I'm a liar

A decay-er of everything I stand for

A voyeur in the dark

An adulterer of the heart

I'm a traitor

A traitor

I committed to be faithful

To keep my passion only for her

Now I'm surfing while she's sleeping

Trusting that our bed is still pure

I've taken what was intimate

And carelessly polluted it

CHORUS

I feel like I'm drowning

Out of control

Like an addict who needs a fix

Selling my soul for the counterfeit high

In these pictures and pixels

God I want to pray to you

But it feels like you wouldn't want me to

CHORUS

DISCUSS (5-10 minutes)

IMAGINE that these lyrics were written by one of your leaders or staff members about himself. How would your organization or ministry probably view that? (For example: a tragedy . . . betrayal . . . an embarrassment . . . a grounds for being disqualified or fired . . . a sign of spiritual immaturity or wickedness . . . not any of our organization's business . . . an opportunity . . . something else?)

PART 2 (90 minutes)

PREVIEW (2 minutes)

ASK someone to read aloud this brief preview:

The implications and consequences of pornography on persons, marriages, and families should be pretty obvious by now. Less recognized are the implications and costs of pornography use in the workplace. Various studies and surveys conducted across the world in the last ten years paint a stark picture of just how much work time employees are devoting to viewing pornography—instead of working. Here are some sample statistics:

- *70% of all on-line porn traffic occurs during the 9-5 workday*
- *2/3 of human resource professionals have discovered porn on employee computers*
- *Half of workers said they had been exposed to sexually explicit material by co-workers*
- *In one month, 44% of U.S. workers admitted to accessing X-rated material at work in one month (compared to 40% of home users)*
- *75% of employees have had porn appear on their computer at work*
- *Managers and leaders reports increased time dealing with porn at work*

So what? If so many of us are spending so much work time viewing porn, what are the harmful consequences? Some of the more obvious impacts in the working world are:

- *Lost productivity*
- *Impact on human resources*

- *Employee well being*
- *Unhealthy work environment*
- *Company reputation and brand*

Though challenging, this situation isn't hopeless. "Every addiction begins with a soft choice, a quiet compromise." You might also say that freedom begins in just the opposite way: "All freedom begins with a hard choice, a refusal to compromise." Part 2 will explore this hope.

WATCH VIDEO (24 minutes)

VIEW the second half of the *Somebody's Daughter* video (from 23:40 to 46:00 End). Use the outline below to take notes on particular things that touch you or that you would like to discuss later.

EXPOSED

Why must we tell somebody about it—for the man and for his wife?

- Strips men and women of dignity; tempts her to leave

- Makes her doubt that what they had together was ever real; everything feels fake and artificial; "Was I believing a lie? I didn't know who he really was."

- What he feels as shame ("I'm not getting close to you because you're purer than I am ... Please forgive me") she reads as rejection ("He doesn't want me ... I'm not sexy enough ... he's rejecting me.")

- She needs to know that it's NOT: "I'm being rejected...I'm not enough ... he doesn't find me

- attraction ... I'm not what he needs or wants" ⇒ feels defeated and wants to run away

- Myth to think he can control this on his own

- Core self-centered demand: I want all of my needs met—apart from God. That is the core element of sinfulness (wickedness) speaking.

- She's embarrassed, he's afraid, so nobody talks about it. Convinces him he's the only one struggling.

- Why must we tell somebody about it?
    - It needs to cause a major disruption in his life
    - Obsession with porn thrives in secrecy
    - Exposing it offers accountability and resources; he will need help walking through this
    - Without exposure, people sink deeper and deeper into darkness.

RELIEVED

How does "coming into the light" bring relief?

- Speaking the truth with his own mouth helps him find a way out. Exposure → Relief → Freedom → Journey → Peace

- Sexual sin loses its power when exposed ... begins to break strongholds

- He needs help, someone he can trust and call

- Wife also needs someone to support her

- Not just accountability, but heart-accessibility
- Not just a cop or a coach, but find a cardiologist (someone concerned about the condition of the heart who will care, pursue, and probe)
- Count the Cost: the years of shame, lost opportunities, and wasted time. The Goal: to bring all this to an end
- Find community /people who care for you, who pursue you, who probe your heart (not just your behavior)
- Commit to becoming free; commit to fight this.
- Draw the line for next generation; they will run where we stumbled. "This is the end! It stops here!"
- Go in with a battle mindset; determine not to be defiled/destroyed by the culture
- Decide not to be defiled by the culture and to do things differently ONLY by God's power
- Trust God to give you new eyes and new mindset

FREED

How do we experience Gospel transformation?

- Beware of approaches that re-shame
- Jesus loves you radically and relentlessly at the expense of His own heart
- Jesus never shames you—even at your worst

- God takes your failures, sins, shame, wickedness, wounds to the cross—and transforms you.

- The cross is about more than forgiveness: also about entering into real life with God.

- Sets you free to love and live with your heart fully alive.

- God has to be bigger than this. There IS hope!

- Struggler: "God, I bring you my nothing." God: "All that is I made out of nothing. Today brings a whole new life for you!"

- Struggler: "God, this is so hard." God: "I know, but I am with you."

- Wife: "I don't have the right to hang on to my resentment because I was wronged."

- Struggler: "Lord, I feel so ashamed and guilty and ugly. I can't stand myself!" God: "My grace is sufficient for you."

- Gospel transformation doesn't have 3 easy steps. It's about letting God transform your perspective and give you entirely new values.

- The Freedom Cry (from David): *"Show me Your ways, O Lord, that I can run in the paths set for me."* (Psalm 119:32 NIV)

Discuss Video (10-15 minutes)

1. What are one or two things from the video that stood out to you?

2. How has this video impacted your perspective on your organization or ministry's response to porn users among you?

3. What if the porn strugglers among you stay hidden—avoid exposure? How will this impact them and the organization?

DISCUSS POSSIBLE REALITIES (20-25 minutes)

1. In light of what you are learning, how would you like to be able to describe (in a few words) your organization or ministry's policy toward porn strugglers?

2. Personally, when a person is addicted to porn, it costs a lot—financially, relationally, emotionally, spiritually, perhaps even physically or legally. Organizationally, there are two kinds of costs: the costs of actively and intentionally helping strugglers versus the costs of ignoring the problem or simply firing them. Try to identify several of the costs that concern you most.

3. For every porn struggler in your midst, several other people are impacted negatively, too (co-workers, supervisors, spouses, clients, etc.). What resources does your organization have (or need) to address the needs of these people experiencing "collateral damage"?

4. What are the questions that your organization or ministry needs to ask and answer in order to develop a redemptive, restorative response to porn strugglers?

LISTEN (5 minutes)

WATCH "Free" music video, by John Mandeville. (4:31 minutes).
© 2005 Lifestyle of Worship (Administered by the Copyright Company) ASCAP / Lifestyle of Worship BMI

Free

Words and Music by John Mandeville

I'm not fighting anymore
I stopped trying
Yeah I've burned all the ammunition
That kept me at war
I'm not weary anymore
I've stopped trying
Trying to live up to expectations
That weren't even mine

I'm free
Finally free
Oh I'm free from the pain and confusion
Thought I'd never be
Yeah I'm free
So free

Made my way through the lies and delusion
To this sweet release
I'm free

I'm not tortured anymore
Got no secrets
I've come clean with the dark obsessions
That haunted my life

I'm not lonely anymore
I've stopped hiding
Yeah I've opened my heart to the passion
That burns in your eyes

CHORUS

And I can't explain
What you've done for me baby
With a love that dared to believe
With a love that really believes

DISCUSS MUSIC TOGETHER (5 minutes)

1. What impact might it have within your organization or ministry if the porn strugglers in your midst stayed on the job or returned to work as men genuinely restored and freed from their addiction?

CHECK OUT (5 minutes)

- What is one concrete step you intend to take when you get back to your organization or ministry in terms of responding to porn among your staff? (Consider beginning to create or amend a policy, designing training for staff, creating an acceptable Internet use policy, etc.)

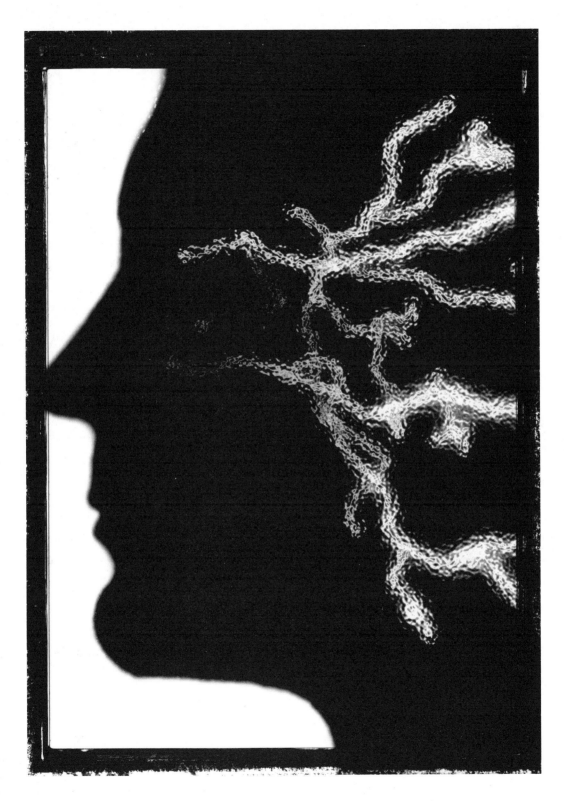

Your Brain on Porn:
seven facts you need to know

I [Michael] will never forget the time a man said to me, "I know it's not really true, but I feel as if my brain has been conditioned by porn." When I asked him why he thought it wasn't true, he told me that to acknowledge such a thing would be shirking personal responsibility. For the next few hours I eagerly shared what I had been learning about the brain and pornography. It seemed as if a heavy load had been lifted off his shoulders.

The fact of the matter is that this man's brain really had been conditioned by porn. And years of sincere effort had been thwarted by a lack of information about pornography's impact on the brain. Like so many others, he wrongly concluded that he was just morally weak and undisciplined.

Since the original release of *Somebody's Daughter* DVD, the scientific notion of neuroplasticity—the idea that the brain can change and be shaped by our behavior—has become a universally accepted fact. Even further, it is an increasingly accepted fact that viewing pornography—from a single instance to regular long-term use—generates significant changes in the brain.

Here is how one brain expert described what happens to a person's brain when viewing a pornographic image:

> "Instantaneously an overpowering flood of chemicals is released in the brain.[1] The viewer probably feels arousal and fear, lust and shock,

---

[1] Mark B. Kastleman, *The Drug of the New Millennium: The Science of How Internet Pornography Radically Alters the Human Brain and Body* (Orem, UT: Granite, 2001).

> *excitement and shame—in a confusing blend that amounts to an emotional-chemical cocktail. These chemicals virtually shut down the frontal lobes, containing the logic center of the brain—the part of the brain that would normally say, Wait a minute . . . are you sure you want to do this? The viewer's cognitive thought and reasoning abilities are overridden by the emotional gut-reaction part of the brain called the limbic system. So the pleasure/emotional center of the brain literally takes over. That exposure to porn lodges itself as an emotional memory before the viewer can take measures to stop it. No wonder a porn viewer often asks himself in bewilderment afterward, What was I thinking? (p. 53)*

Maybe you can relate to the bewildered feeling of "what was I thinking?" Or maybe you've heard someone else describe this experience. Either way, no discussion of sexual compulsion is complete without a basic discussion of how porn alters the brain, creating addiction. It is our hope that by being armed with this information you will be better equipped to engage in the battle for your heart.

Fact #1   Porn is a drug.

Over the years I've heard countless men say, "Porn isn't really addictive . . . at least not in the same way as cocaine, pills, or alcohol." If no chemical is ingested into the body then addiction cannot occur, they say. But nothing could be further from the truth.

In recent years, numerous studies have shown that behavioral addictions like pornography can affect the brain in all the same ways as substance addictions. This means the brain of a man who regularly uses porn can be changed so that his brain pathways come to resemble those of a drug addict or alcoholic.

Knowing that porn is a drug and can be just as addictive as nicotine, pills, cocaine, or meth can be a game changer during recovery. Knowing porn is a drug shifts the nature of the battle and reframes the struggle. It's no longer simply a matter of moral weakness or faithlessness. At some point the struggle comes down to pathways and chemicals in your brain. A basic understanding of these provides a context for why you can't stop doing something that deep down you really don't want to do.

Fact # 2   Porn has harmful consequences.

Another thing I've heard men say over the years is, "What's the big deal? Porn isn't so harmful is it?" But now that you know porn is a drug, you won't be surprised to learn that it comes with potentially negative consequences that you might expect from the abuse of a drug.

In numerous studies, men who regularly used porn report decreased self-confidence and self-esteem, as well as increased depression and loneliness. These men describe being less passionate and less engaged with life in general. On the relational and social front they are more isolated, and less likely to initiate romantic relationships.

Porn addiction also results in troubling physical symptoms. More and more men, including men in their early twenties, are experiencing sexual performance difficulties like erectile dysfunction and the inability to be sexually aroused in the presence of a "real woman."

Fact #3   Porn hijacks the brain.

Speaking of serious negative consequences, regular porn use can hijack the brain chemistry. It can affect what we want and how much we want. Ever heard of a chemical called dopamine? It's a chemical in the brain known as the "gotta have it" molecule. Dopamine is the neurotransmitter associated with pleasure and reward. It's the gas for our desire engine. Imagine eating at a favorite restaurant or going on vacation. Just the thought of these pleasures causes the brain to release dopamine. The more intense and powerful an experience, the more dopamine is released. The issue with online porn is that too much dopamine is released. The brain is over-stimulated, and, according to brain expert, Dr. William Struthers, our brains are hijacked. This happens for four distinct reasons.

The first reason why porn hijacks our brain is that the brain craves novelty. With online porn, novel images are instantly available. With every new image the brain releases a burst of dopamine, telling us we "gotta have it." A man can view new and ever more stimulating images without leaving the computer. Because dopamine is fueling the desire engine, as long as novel images continue, arousal will continue.

A second reason why online porn over-stimulates the brain is that supplies of the pornographic images are virtually unlimited. With substance addictions a person eventually runs out of the drug or they are unable to tolerate more. But with only an Internet connection a man can continue to binge.

A third reason Internet porn over-stimulates the brain has to do with tolerance. This eventually occurs in any addiction when a person needs more and more of the drug to reach the same pleasurable reward. In the case of drug or food addictions, this means consuming more frequently or consuming larger amounts. As tolerance for the drug increases so does frustration because the "payoff" is no longer as rewarding. With online porn, the tolerance effect can be overcome in two ways. One way is to increase the amount of time viewing porn. Another is to escalate the intensity of the onscreen images by seeking images that shock, repel, or disgust.

The fourth reason porn over-stimulates the brain is that it's on demand. Where a drug user has to arrange for a fix, the memory holds a perpetual stash of images that don't even require a computer. Just because you log off the computer doesn't mean the images cease to exist. Just by bringing an image to mind, the brain releases more dopamine.

By combining these four dopamine-stimulating factors, online porn generates a perfect storm in the neurochemical sea of the brain. In fact, if some malevolent being were to attempt to create the perfect delivery mechanism for enslaving human desire, online porn would win the prize.

Fact #4   Porn rewires and changes the brain.

So online porn over-stimulates the brain by releasing too much dopamine. The real problem is set in motion, however, because the brain then adapts to being over-stimulated. Adapting causes the brain to change and rewire itself in three ways. The first of these changes result in cravings—intense physical urges to view more porn. Cravings occur as dopamine is released. Typically, cravings lead to viewing more porn, which leads to more dopamine release, which leads to more craving, which leads to viewing more porn. You get the idea. It's a vicious cycle of frustration where the brain wants porn more and more, but likes it less and less. It's like always being hungry, but eating and never feeling full.

The second change in the brain affects the reward circuit between the part of the brain controlling urges and desires ("go for it"), and the logical rational part of the brain ("think about it"). Ideally this reward circuit works in harmony—when urges beckon—the rational brain evaluates whether it's a good idea. But porn trips the circuit breaker. Because the "go for it" part of the brain is over-stimulated with excess dopamine, the "think about it" system reacts to system overload and shuts down. On a neurochemical level it's a case of increased urge and decreased judgment.

The third change is known as a numbed pleasure response. If dopamine is too high for too long, nerve cells lose ability to communicate. Think about it this way: nerve cells sending dopamine are screaming ("More dopamine!"), while the receiving nerve cells cover their ears. So the sending cells scream louder until they lose their voice and can only whisper (level of dopamine sent is below normal). The receiving cells are now virtually deaf and the sending cells can only whisper. Ultimately, too much of a good thing creates an inability to enjoy the good thing.

Fact #5   Porn creates an addicted brain.

As the brain adapts because of too much dopamine it becomes addicted. Left with feeling awful or viewing more porn, in one sense regular porn users become addicted to their own brain chemistry. No wonder counselors and addiction experts call porn "visual crack cocaine."

Everything we do, think, and feel has a corresponding pathway in the brain. As the brain's reward circuits struggle for harmony, the brain rewires itself by creating new pathways. And every time a man views another pornographic image, the dopamine burst strengthens connections between pathways. Whatever the behavior we do, the more we use a brain pathway, the stronger the pathway becomes.

Think of the pathways in your brain as footpaths of waist high grass. When the grass is high it requires effort to walk the path. But every time you walk along the path, it takes less effort. Eventually, it becomes a dirt path. Addiction not only causes the grass to wear down, but it also works like a weed eater cutting through the tall grass.

And despite your best intentions, you lack resistance to stop yourself.

As I will discuss below, the grass can grow back. Your brain pathways can be rewired.

Fact #6   Porn addicted brains can be rewired to health.

Just as a computer can be rebooted to reset the hard drive, your brain can be rebooted and reset to healthy functioning. It's like giving your brain a "time out" so it can begin to regain balance. Some addicted brain circuits may be restored to health in as little as ninety days. For the best possible outcome, follow these guidelines below.

Prepare

Define Your Objective

Research suggests that those who prepare for significant behavioral changes are less likely to relapse than those who impulsively initiate change with little or no preparation. The first way to prepare for the change you are about to make is to define an objective.

Expect Withdrawal Symptoms

In the case of rebooting your brain from pornography, preparation includes being aware that you may suffer withdrawal symptoms. Although temporary, withdrawal symptoms can include fatigue, depression, difficulty concentrating, nervousness, sleeplessness, headaches, changes in appetite, rapid heartbeat, and shortness of breath. Knowing that these symptoms are normal is good information to have during the reboot.

Anticipate Cravings

A final preparation before rebooting is to anticipate cravings—intense physical desires for pornography occurring during the initial ninety days. These powerful physical sensations draw you to the "drug," but usually last no more than a few weeks. Finally, remind yourself that cravings are not an indication as to what's true about your heart. The fact is cravings are the direct result of your brain being over-stimulated.

Choose a Start Date and Begin 90 Days of Abstinence

Choosing a start date gives you time to prepare, allows you to track progress, and helps you stay motivated. One of the tools I suggest, beginning on day one of the ninety-day reboot, is purchasing two inexpensive decks of playing cards. First, randomly count out ninety cards. On day one flip the top card over as a symbol of you learning to live life without pornography. Each new day you flip a new card until you go through the deck of ninety cards. In the event that you relapse, don't start over with the cards—keep going forward.

Although it's entirely counterintuitive, don't focus on how many days you log without looking at pornography. Instead of putting energy and focus into what you are not doing, put your focus toward what you are doing. It's more about what you are moving toward, and less about what you are leaving behind. Rebooting is about letting grass grow back on the pathways in your brain. So each day, when you flip one of the ninety cards, picture a worn down path beginning to sprout higher and higher.

Fact #7 Porn addiction can be overcome—there is hope!

The story of God revealed in the scriptures is that he is making all things new through Jesus (Isaiah 43:19). No matter how deep or how long you have struggled, God longs to make all things new in you. He has already made a way for you. There is hope for real change. As you take the next steps on your journey or restoration, we recommend a plan that includes five "R's," each representing different steps along the path to freedom.

Recognize

The first part of recognition is identifying—giving something a name. And men are famous for euphemisms. We often use these to avoid the ugly truth. So don't say you are having "purity issues," "moral struggles," or "lust issues." Call it what it is—compulsive sexual sin, enslavement, bondage, addiction.

The second aspect of recognizing is acceptance. Not to be confused with resignation or giving up, acceptance is coming to terms that the addiction is not going away on its own. Remember Jesus saying, " . . . the truth will set you free" (John 8:32)? Identifying and accepting the problem is nothing more than truth telling. Sometimes the truth we need to speak out loud is to ourselves, and other times we need to speak it to someone else.

Reach out

Allow me to be blunt. If you want to be free struggling alone is not optional. Healing and recovery are not a solo journey. Porn addiction is all about isolation. We stare at the screen and we are alone. We carry our shame and we are alone. We listen to the lies in our head and we are alone. Ultimately, the antidote to porn addiction is connection—to our own heart, to God's merciful heart, and to the heart of another.

The benefits of reaching out and asking for help are many. Our secrets lose their power. We are known and loved for who we really are. God rewards humility. You will have accountability. So reach out to a friend, mentor, pastor, or counselor.

Repent

What is the first thing that comes to mind when you hear the word "repentance?" Do you think of words like remorse, guilt, or feeling terrible about a sin? Do you think of an intense commitment or sincere intention to not repeat certain sins? If so, you are like many men who misunderstand repentance as it relates to the battle with pornography.

In Psalm 51, after committing adultery with Bathsheba, David repented. His repentance centered on his realization that God didn't want more religious activity—sacrifices and burnt offerings. What David realized was that God wanted David to trust Him with his whole heart.

The biblical meaning of the word repentance is to change directions. To choose a different path. To do life differently. What does this look like? It's the man who gets caught in the porn trap and "repents" by reaching out instead of struggling alone. It's the man who "repents" by confessing his struggle with intimacy, not just his sin. It's the man who "repents" by confessing his self-sufficiency, even though he doesn't know any other way to live.

Reboot

Computers can be rebooted to reset their hard drive. In the same way, a man's brain can be rebooted to reset his brain from the default setting of porn. In short, rebooting involves a beginning a minimum ninety-day period without viewing pornography or masturbating. During this time, the brain resets itself.

Rebooting is entirely different from previous attempts you might have made to stop viewing porn. Where past attempts have been about controlling your will or suppressing desire, rebooting puts the emphasis on your brain being changed. Your emphasis is on putting new brain pathways in place, not keeping porn away.

For more information on rebooting your brain, to read a free chapter of "Your Brain On Porn," and to download a free Reboot Kit, visit www.surfingforgodbook.com

Reorient

Porn disorients us. It makes us lose our bearings as to what's truly important. We lose our connection to our true heart. Many men who reboot report an experience like waking up to a new life. As the brain begins to return to a healthy non-addicted state you may begin to feel confidence and courage to risk new experiences and relationships.

Reorientation is a time of learning how to connect more authentically with God, your own heart, and others. During this time true intimacy—in real relationships—begins to override the false intimacy of porn.

Questions for Reflection and Discussion:

1. Is this information about the brain and pornography new to you? What parts had you heard before?

2. Which of the seven facts about your brain on porn stand out to you? Why?

3. How does knowing this information affect how you approach this struggle (whether in your own life or someone you know)?

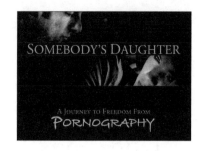

"I was looking at pornography every day and it was slowly destroying my marriage. I was on the verge of losing everything. One day my two teenage sons sat me down and said. "Dad, we got this DVD and we want you to watch it with us. It was the Somebody's Daughter *documentary. I had no idea that they realized how bad my problem was.*

As I sat there and watched with them the dam just broke. Here were my sons protecting their mom and confronting me with the truth. Somebody's Daughter *gave them a way to get my attention...and it certainly did. Watching that documentary is what made me realize I was not alone and needed to get help.*

I did and am happy to share that my marriage is in the best shape it has been in in years. I am not looking at pornography anymore.

This would not have happened without Somebody's Daughter. *I urge anyone struggling with this issue to get a copy."*

~ Winston, Husband & Father, now living in freedom

The six time award-winning DVD/documentary *Somebody's Daughter: A Journey to Freedom from Pornography* focuses on raising awareness of the pervasiveness and destructiveness of pornography as it features the struggle of Christians - it's a testimony that this effects Christians and non-Christians alike. The spoken testimonies and songs speak to the hearts of the men, women, husbands and wives - the victims - being oppressed by this insidious industry.

The DVD/CD set also contains four music videos and eight vignettes. The powerful CD contains 9 original songs, stories, poetry, and scripture readings.

TO ORDER your *Somebody's Daughter* DVD/CD set or additional copies of this guide please visit: http://www.musicforthesoul.org/resources/somebodys-daughter/

inquire@musicforthesoul.org
Music for the Soul
P.O. Box 159027
Nashville, TN 37215-9027

RESOURCES

For ways to get involved in helping create a culture that values the dignity and worth of every human being visit www.shessomebodysdaughter.org

RESOURCES RELATED TO THE BRAIN

Surfing For God: Discovering The Divine Desire Beneath Sexual Struggle.

www.surfingforgodbook.com

Wired for Intimacy, William Struthers, PhD

This book is written by a neuroscientist with a Christian worldview and provides an understandable, yet in-depth exploration of how God designed our brains for connection and intimacy, and how porn diminishes this capacity.

www.yourbrainonporn.com

This website is run by neuroscientist Gary Wilson, who interprets scientific research, posts popular articles, and facilitates discussion around the brain and pornography. Although Wilson takes no moral stand against pornography, he passionately labors to help men understand how porn rewires the brain in disturbing ways.

Suggested Uses for Additional CD and Video Content

Songs

"All of Me" This song challenges us to "come clean" and let go of our "favorite" sins, surrendering them to God. Play this song and then discuss the concept of favorite sins and what that says about our sinful nature.

"I Commit My Eyes" In this song men are encouraged to make a promise to God about how they will use their eyes in order to overcome the onslaught of sexual imagery in today's culture. Play the song and then ask men to give specific examples of ways they might "commit" their eyes.

"Every Man's Battle" This song encourages the listener to find accountability partners in order to stay the course of the higher road toward sexual purity. Have men split off into pairs and talk honestly with one another about what they are learning from the group and then set some new goals.

For Youth

"Losing Ground" VIDEO Our youth are growing up in an evermore highly sexualized culture. This song talks frankly about one young man's frustration as he fights to overcome the temptations that arise from being bombarded by sexual imagery. He ultimately turns to Jesus as the way to "end the shame." Play the song for your youth group. And ask them if they can identify with Topher's struggle. What kind of "lies" come at them regarding sexuality? Discuss the tension and peer pressure young people feel about sexuality, living both as people of faith and as citizens of the world. Talk about what trusting Jesus looks like for them with regard to attitudes toward sex.

SPOKEN WORD

Throughout the CD there are personal testimonies, poetry, and interviews. These pieces lend the authenticity of human experience to the project. Scripture is also included to bring the authority of God. Use these different elements to prompt discussion.

"The Lies of the Eyes" This poem describes the devastation brought upon one man's life by always keeping his struggle with pornography a secret. Discuss the consequences of his hiding this part of his life. Ask the group members if they have ever had a secret that caused more and more problems the longer it was kept hidden.

"Two Different Me's" In this brief testimony one man shares his pain living a double life. Have members of the group share a time have they've felt as if an area of their private life was at odds with their public life.

"Disgusting" This man talks about how he felt when he realized that other men could be looking at his daughter the same way he was looking at other women. Then we hear a "gallows" laugh. What do you think the man was feeling when he laughed? Ask group members to share how it makes them feel to think of other men looking with lust at their daughter, wife, sister, or other woman they love.

"I Tell You" Several scriptures are woven together here to share a biblical perspective on sexuality. Ask group members to select one of the scriptures shared by the pastor and talk about what they think it means for their own walk.

"A Difficult Confession" Have the group listen to Renee's story. If there are any women in the group, ask them to share which parts of Renee's story resonate for them.

Ask the men in the group to share how hearing Renee's story might make them more or less likely to be truthful with their wives.

"Bounce" Fred Stoeker outlines a discipline he developed to help him not dwell on women as sex objects. Is this a practical solution? Ask men in the group what has worked for them?

"Open Up Your Life" Bernie talks in this piece about how important it is to open up and to keep talking regularly and honestly with other men about what is going on in your life. Challenge your men to set up a regular weekly one-on-one meeting with someone else in group. If there are women in your group, encourage them to set up an ongoing support group.

"You Can Make It" John summarizes in one presentation the story he tells on the VIDEO. Ask the group members to talk about what parts of John's story give them hope. What does his story challenge them to do differently?

Related Resources for

Men/Young Adults:

Restoring the Soul Ministry: http://www.restoringthesoul.org

http://surfingforGodbook.com

Into the Light Ministries: http://intothelightministries.net/

Covenant Eyes: http://covenanteyes.com/pornstats

XXX Church: http://www.xxxchurch.com/men/

Women/Wives/Young Adults:

http://www.shessomebodysdaugher.org

No Stones: Women Redeemed from Sexual Shame: http://www.amazon.com/No-Stones-Women-Redeemed-Sexual/dp/1591600162

Dirty Girls Come Clean: http://www.dirtygirlsministries.com

XXX Church: http://www.xxxchurch.com/women/

http://route1520.com

http://mygracejourney.com

Faithful and True: http://www.faithfulandtrue.com

Shattered Vows: Hope and Healing for Women Who Have Been Sexually Betrayed: http://www.amazon.com/Shattered-Vows-Healing-Sexually-Betrayed/dp/0310273943

http://www.bethesdaworkshops.org

Studies on Transformation

CONNECT series
Home page: http://bit.ly/NyPHfT

GOD: Connecting with His Outrageous Love - http://bit.ly/MGgQez

IDENTITY: Becoming Who God Says I Am - http://bit.ly/NHonJe

SOUL: Embracing My Sexuality and Emotions - http://bit.ly/Obsy3K

FREEDOM: Breaking the Power of Shame - http://bit.ly/cvCAMa

RELATIONSHIPS: Bringing Jesus Into My World - http://bit.ly/Lq3JwS

LIFE: Thriving in a Complex World - http://bit.ly/MrCk03

*Free downloadable Leader's Guides available for each study

Somebody's Daughter DVD/CD set or additional copies of this guide please visit:
http://www.musicforthesoul.org/resources/somebodys-daughter/